# Ultimate
# Sheet Metal Fabrication

Timothy Remus

Published by:
Wolfgang Publications Inc.
PO Box 10
Scandia, MN 55073

First published in 1999 by Wolfgang Publications Inc., P.O. Box 10, Scandia, MN 55073, USA.

ISBN number: 0 9641358 9 2

Printed and bound in the USA

On the cover: The roadster in raw aluminum is the RRR Special crafted by Steve Moal and his number one "wheel man" Jimmy Kilroy. The craftsman on the English wheel is well-known fabricator Ron Covell.

Ultimate

# Sheet Metal Fabrication

# Acknowledgements

It's that time again. I just spoke with my printer and promised to have half the book over to them by Monday. That means three days to finish up all the items on the "missing" list. At the top of that list (it's alphabetical) is the Acknowledgements.

Some would call them artists and some would call them craftsmen. I call them metal fabricators. Regardless the label each is creative, clever and driven. Largely self-taught, these individuals succeed largely through their own initiative and perseverance.

I find them all fascinating and owe them a large debt of gratitude. Each welcomed me into their shop and spent the better part of a day fabricating parts for the camera. Steve Davis, one of the best known fabricators in the country, is a good example of the breed. More fame and phone calls are probably not what he needs. Yet he always welcomes me to his shop out of a desire to share with others a life time's worth of skills.

Ron Covell makes his living fabricating and teaching others how to fabricate. Working with Ron was a pleasure as he fully understands the need for good light, lots of photographs, and time spent in explanations.

Bo Olson is a "local," his shop is in Stillwater, Minnesota, not far from where I live. This means I can enjoy his skills and kindness by jumping into the truck instead of onto an airplane. Like all the others, Bo took the better part of a day to explain for the camera the work of creating parts that can't be purchased in any dealership or NAPA store.

Neal Letourneau is a talented young man, able to weld and so much more. Though he currently holds down a "day job" the growing number of enthusiasts beating a path to his door may soon force Neal to join the ranks of the self employed.

Bob Munroe works out of a small shop behind his house. He's always apologizing for the small shop and lack of big, fancy tools. Yet, the shapes Bob creates are as lovely as any I've seen.

John Reed's shop starts in the attached garage (the cars sit outside) and spills over into an ever-increasing series of sheds and outbuildings. The current project at John's might be an intriguing one-off V-twin, or a gravity powered street-luge. No matter what it is, it's shaped from metal with John's very talented hands.

Marcel De Ley and his sons, Luc and Marc, work behind the scenes. Many of the hand-built hot rods to come out of the big brand name California shops are actually built largely at Marcel's shop, though they seldom get credit for the job.

Loren Richards is the man who introduced me to Cass Nawrocki. Cass in turn showed me the wide range of shapes that can be created with some simple built-in-shop tooling.

For layout I have to thank Julie Hansen. And in closing I must once again thank my lovely and talented wife, Mary Lanz, for both proofreading and patience.

# Introduction

During my work on the *Ultimate American Hot Rod* book I was lucky enough to meet Steve Moal and see the wonderful RRR Special during construction. Though I've admired fabricators and tin smiths for years and years, the work being done in Steve Moal's shop was like a light bulb going on. While we applaud old-world skills and hand built products, most of what we buy comes from huge factories. Digital watches, cell phones and laptop computers come off assembly lines at the rate of hundreds or thousands per hour. Each one cased in unbreakable, perfectly formed, gray plastic.

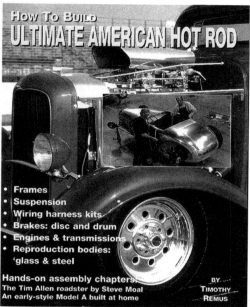

Amidst all this haste there exists a small group of (mostly) men who are trying to slow down just enough to slip into their small shops and learn how to build a patch panel for the Model A or air cleaner for the V-twin.

Though book publishing is a profit driven venture (I've got to have my cell phones too) some projects are more enjoyable than others. It's been my great pleasure to spend considerable time with some of the best tin-smiths in the country. This book is my attempt to assemble their considerable collective wisdom and make it available to those individuals trying to find an extra hour to sneak out into the garage and make that first air cleaner – by hand.

The projects included here range from the simple to the complex. From a "blower scoop" to a two part motorcycle fender. Some will make a good first-time project while others require a bit more experience to duplicate. In each case I've tried to let the fabricator tell the story through quotes and interviews.

Describing the endless subtle changes that occur to a piece of steel as it goes from a "flat sheet" to a "finished fender," is difficult no matter who's telling the story. Thus I've chosen to use more photos and less text (as compared to most of the other Wolfgang books) and let the photos tell much of the story.

Among all the very experienced craftsmen who helped with this book there are a few things they all agree on: First, you don't need a lot of big fancy tools to get started. Second, though books are great (especially this one) metal shaping is one of those skills that is best learned through hands-on experience.

There's a lot of information here which I hope you find useful in building both your own skills and some really bitchin' fenders, air cleaners or hood scoops.

## Chapter One

# Planning and Mock Up

## Think First

How much time you spend in planning a project, before picking up the tin snips, will depend largely on the project itself. If your intent is to replace an existing fender on an old Packard or a panel on a Biplane then there isn't any pressing need for elaborate sketches and renderings. If, on the other hand, your intent is to build a one-off fender for that latest Harley-Davidson project the planning becomes a much bigger part of the job.

Whether you need drawings, and how elabo-

*The California Special is the car that inspired Tim Allen to commission Steve Moal to construct the RRR Special.*

*Like all big projects, this one started with a series of drawings and then a final rendering.*

rate those renderings should be, depends on the project. Fabricator Steve Moal explains that the first step in building the Tim Allen roadster was the call he made to artist Don Varner. "We had to start with the (earlier) California Special. That was the car Tim reacted to. Don Varner worked up a set of drawings that we presented to Tim Allen to get his reactions. Based on those reactions we came up with a final rendering. We tried to key into the things he really liked. The whole process is a way to test design concepts."

*This is one in a series of renderings that Don Varner did for Steve Moal, to be presented to Tim Allen. The more complex the project, the more important the renderings become.*

Once Tim approved the shape Steve asked Don for a full-size set of drawings. And based on those drawings Steve and his crew could start on the actual building.

As Steve Moal explains, that one-off custom project probably needs to start with a good sketch that includes dimensions. If you're building motorcycle sheet metal for an existing chassis, then you can start with an enlarged photo of the chassis, a straight side view, and sketch the sheet metal shapes on tracing paper laid over the chassis photo. If what you're building is a motorcycle fender then your design needs to include the location and design of the support brackets and struts as well.

Whether you build a one-off fender or a replacement part, most of the larger and more elaborate projects will require a three dimen-

*The Tim Allen car near completion. In spite of the renderings some things did change as the car neared completion. In particular, Steve didn't like the rear body section once it was on the car and cut it all off to start over. Steve stresses the importance of rolling the vehicle outside occasionally during the construction so you can get back far enough to truly assess the shapes.*

*Before constructing the rear fender for the Arlen Ness Arrow bike Bob Munroe made a pretty elaborate buck. Bob Munroe*

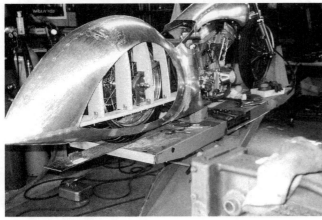

*Farther along in the project. You can see here how Bob laid the aluminum right over the buck. Bob Munroe*

*The finished and hand-built machine. Though the front and rear fenders were crafted with the help of a buck, Bob did the entire gas tank without a buck.*

sional buck or checking device. As Steve Davis explains, "Without that form (or buck), you don't have a way to settle the shape - you keep working and working and it's real frustrating. Sometimes the project changes as you go along, but you still need the plan."

Many sheet metal fabricators like to create the part in paper before the fabrication actually begins. This "paper" stage includes the creation of the part from light board. The idea is to build the air cleaner or dash or small sheet metal part from individual pieces of light board. After you like the size and shape of the new part, you can cut the tape holding the mock up together and use the individual pieces of board as templates for cutting the sheet metal.

More elaborate fabrication projects, especially one-off parts, often require the fabrication of a true buck before the bending can begin. In most cases (there are always exceptions) the buck is only a checking device, the forming is done on the bench or on the shrinker, and then the progress can be checked against the buck.

The buck itself can be built from wood in the traditional fashion, or from Styrofoam or the new Jiffy foam often used for prototyping parts.

With the buck finished, most fabricators include another step before they begin the actual tin work. A piece of paper draped over the buck can be used as a means of determining how much shaping must be done to duplicate the curves of the sketch. Where the paper bunches up you'll have too much metal, necessitating some shrinking. And where the paper won't reach without being slit you know some stretching will be in order. You can even plan out how many pieces of metal it will take to cover the buck, and exactly where the seams should be placed. (Note the Steve Davis forming sequence in this chapter.)

Some fabricators use a hammerform. Not to be confused with a buck, the hammerform is used as a mold and the metal is shaped, through both shrinking and stretching, to fit the form (see Chapter Five for more on hammerforms).

## THE POSSIBILITIES ARE NOT ENDLESS

During the planning phase it might pay to recall exactly what you can and can't do with a piece of metal. And which is the easiest to perform. To quote metal-man Ron Covell, "There are only five things you can do to metal: stretch it, shrink it, bend it, cut it or weld it (join it). That's pretty much the end of the story. Everything is made

*Jiffy foam, available at many hobby stores, carves easily to form a buck for that next fabrication project. In order to make it more durable it can be covered with the two-part, light-weight filler seen here.*

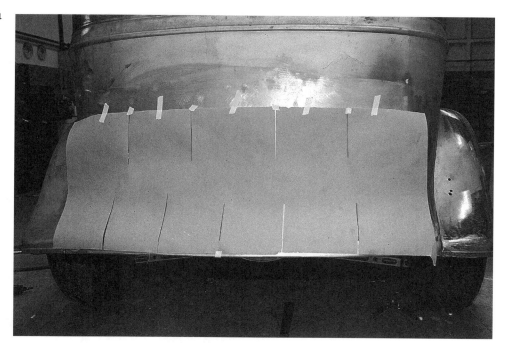

*Seen in the De Ley shop, the rear panel on this Chevy sedan was very difficult to shape. The paper tells the story, on both the top and bottom the metal had to stretch, while along the center it actually had to shrink.*

9

# Paper Predicts The Project

The following sequence is part of an earlier Harley-Davidson Sheet Metal book. The part being formed is the front corner of a motorcycle gas tank, one of the Lil' John Billet Bike tanks to be more specific. Of note, the front corner is probably the hardest part of a motorcycle tank to form because it has so much shape. The sequence is presented here as an excellent illustration of both the use of a buck, and the way a piece of paper can be used to give a crystal-ball-like look into the future before starting on a particular piece of sheet metal.

Here he pins the paper to the buck, note the overlap on the various "flaps" of paper.

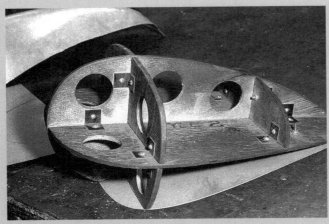

The buck seen here, shaped like the gas tank, is for checking the shape and not for forming. For individuals working at home this could be made from foam.

With the paper pinned to the buck, Steve marks the edge of each overlap with a pencil.

Steve cuts long slits in the paper so the slits can overlap and the paper can be "formed" to the buck.

The amount of overlap at each of the joints indicates how much shrinking the metal will have to do there to match the shape of the buck.

# Paper Predicts The Project

Steve punches holes that mark the "front" of the tank and transfers those to the metal.

The developing tank section is checked often against the buck. At this point it looks pretty good, though the very front of the tank section needs to be stretched.

The punch holes from the paper are made into a line marked on the metal. This is the line the separates the area that needs shrinking from the area that needs stretching.

With a little ATF as lubricant, Steve uses one of his favorite home-made hammers to stretch the area at the front of the tank.

Steve shrinks the outer area, where the flaps of paper overlapped, with the power hammer.

After some finishing work on the planishing hammer, and some filing with a Vixen file, the new tank section is done and ready to weld to the other panels needed to make the entire tank.

*When you get really good at metal crafting try the fabrication of a compete car like this 1937 Mercedes 540K. Built entirely by hand, even the bumpers, by Cass Nawrocki.*

*Most of this body was formed from 19 gauge cold rolled steel, some it was "deep-draw" or aluminum-killed steel sheet. Note the amount of shape in the fenders and the spare tire well. Cass even made the trim for the car.*

through a combination of those processes. Of those five cutting is no big deal, bending is straight forward. Welding is a discipline, something you learn through practice and perseverance..."

"We come to shrinking and stretching, those are the tricky parts of the process. For most people stretching is by far the easiest. You can do it with a hammer and a sand bag. What drives people nuts is the shrinking part of the equation. This is true for amateurs and professionals alike."

Once you get the idea to build a fender, or to create your own patch panels, for the project in the garage the best thing to do is slow down. "The hardest part of the project," says Loren Richards is deciding where to start, how to proceed."

As Loren points out, you have to decide not only whether to stretch or shrink, but which to do first, second, and third. Many of these projects will require that you use more than one panel. But how many? And where should you put the seams so you can get at both sides later for final finishing?

The one thing all the experienced fabricators agreed on was the notion that your first project should be a simple one. Don't try to build a complete Deuce body the first time out. Instead, create some patch panels for the Chevy sedan, or an air cleaner cover for the Harley-Davidson.

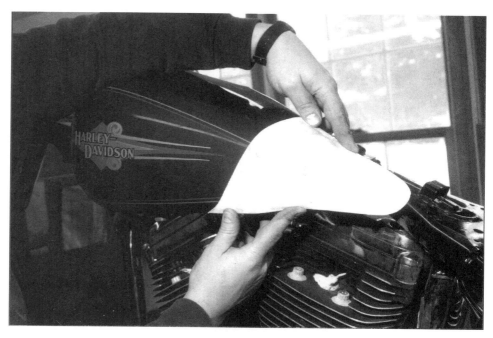

*Even the simplest projects benefit from a paper mock up. Here Rob Roehl fashions a "tail" to extend a Fat Bob gas tank in Donnie Smith's shop.*

*The mock up makes a good template to cut out the steel. Then it's time for some careful shaping, a little welding, and the finish work before painting.*

## Chapter Two

# Tools & Materials

## The right tool for the job

You don't need a tremendous amount of tools to get started with fabricating. As Steve Moal, long-time fabricator and builder of the Tim Allen Roadster, is fond of saying, "...people say the Italian cars are rough, but if you get in there and look at the things they did *without any of the tools that we have today* it's impressive. Not only are the cars beautiful, the craftsmanship is lovely as well. It's the kind of work I'd be proud to call my own."

"You really don't need an awful lot of tools to get

*An English wheel is a great tool, but don't think it's essential. Plenty of very fine cars have been built with only hammers, dollies and maybe a nice tree stump.*

started," adds Steve Davis. "A couple of body hammers with matching dollies, some tin snips, a bag of shot, and maybe some type of soft faced hammer. An assortment of 'garage junk' is always handy as an aid in shaping and forming the panels. Pipes in various sizes can be helpful in forming simple curves and a piece of angle iron can be used as a 'brake' if you clamp it to the bench."

You will also need a ruler and a square, along with a good scribe and possibly a can of bluing (or even dark primer) to make it easier to see the scribed line. A standard fluted drill bit leaves an oblong hole when used on sheet metal. A drill that is "stepped" is a better idea for drilling round holes in sheet metal. Countersink bits allow you to de-burr the hole after you drill it, and can also be used to position that screw head flush with the surface of the sheet metal.

To some degree the amount of tools will depend on your budget, your experience and the type of projects you intend to tackle.

Small brakes for making neat bends in sheet metal are available for a small shop. The tool that nearly every fabricator uses on a regular basis is the shrinker. For the big shops the shrinkers are air powered, while in the smaller shops it's arms or feet that power the shrinker. Many of these are available in small sizes from tool companies like Eastwood and most can be converted to stretchers with a different set of dies.

Experienced (and well funded) builders may use somewhat exotic tools like a

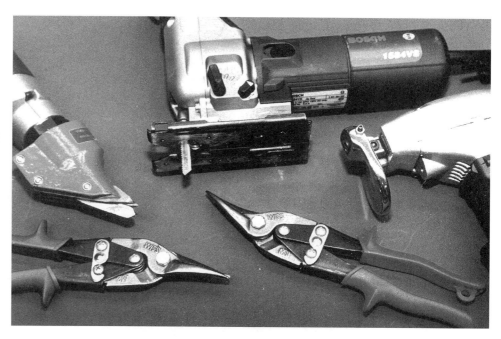

*A variety of means, both power and hand operated, are available for cutting metal. You have to consider how accurate the cut is and how much damage the cutting does to the edge.*

*Dollies come in every imaginable shape. T dollies can be anchored in the vise and used like a specialized anvil. Hand held dollies should have a shape that matches that of the sheet metal they are held up against.*

15

Yoder power hammer or an English wheel. Because of its size the Yoder simply isn't an option for most small shops. A more practical tool for the serious but perhaps amateur fabricator is an English wheel (see the interview with Loren Richards in this chapter). A tool like a power hammer has the advantage of being both a shrinker and a stretcher, while the English wheel is typically only used to stretch the metal.

The types of tools you have in your shop will affect the kinds of jobs you tackle, and how you go about each one. There is nearly always more than one way to form a particular panel. The way you do it, and the exact sequence of operations that you follow,

*Though it isn't elaborate, this would make a pretty good beginning sheet metal working tool kit: two dollies with different shapes, two metal hammers with different amounts of crown on the head, and one or two plastic hammers.*

will be determined in part by the tools in your shop. While the owner of a large hammer has the option of shrinking and stretching, most of us are forced to use stretching for most of the forming necessary to create fenders, side covers and patch panels.

There are a few more specialized tools that you may want to purchase, like the bulls-eye-pick favored by Ron Covell (see Chapter Five) and a Vixen file or two for finish work.

You probably already own a few grinders and possibly a die grinder. Though it might sound obvious, it's probably worth mentioning the damage that a large body grinder can do to a steel or aluminum panel. Most serious metal crafters advise people to stay away from body grinders, the tool Steve Davis called, "one of the worst tools that was ever introduced to the body trade. It wants to go in there and cut groves in the material and it adds a lot of heat. It also work-hardens the metal."

In lieu of a big body grinder most metal craftsmen finish their panels with hammer and dolly, sometimes used in conjunction with a Vixen file. Approved power tools include small grinders, often equipped with a foam pad behind the sanding pad. Those that use small sanders to finish the metal do so with caution, and often use lubricant to avoid over-heating the metal. Some use a die grinder to carefully knock the high spots off a small area like a weld bead.

### SAFETY

Grinders, both large and small, create airborne dust. For all sanding and grinding operations you need at least a dust-filter mask and eye protection. Aluminum dust is especially unhealthy and you should use a charcoal-type face mask for grinding aluminum as well as for any spray painting done in the shop. A pair of leather gloves will help you get a good grip on that piece of sheet metal, prevent cuts to your digits, and minimize fatigue that comes from holding a hammer and dolly in your hands for hours at a time.

Don't forget your ears. Grinders and hammers make a hell of a racket so it's a good idea to keep the hearing protection hanging on a nail close to the work bench.

## MATERIALS

Once you've created the new part from light board, it's time to start cutting, forming and welding. But first you have to determine whether the new part should be made from steel or aluminum.

As always, there are two sides to every argument and every material choice. Steel is easier to buy, weld, and paint. Aluminum on the other hand is softer so it shapes more easily, but it's harder for most of us to paint or weld.

### Steel

For many automotive and motorcycle projects steel is the logical choice. At least two of the craftsmen interviewed in this book, Steve Davis and Bob Monroe, are big believers in a specialized steel sheet known as "drawing-quality" or aluminum-killed steel. This sheet steel is formed by adding a little bit of aluminum at the end of the steel making process. The

*When you pull the handle down the jaws are brought down onto the metal and then forced together.*

*A shrinker is simply a tool that gathers up the metal. Here we see the jaws of a small hand-operated shrinker in the open position.*

aluminum gives the steel it's name and a more malleable nature. You may have to call around to some metal-houses to find this specialized sheet, or ask at a big stamping facility if you can buy some of their excess or scrap (check the Sources section).

If you can't find drawing-quality steel at least buy cold-rolled, not hot-rolled, steel. The cold-rolled sheet is cleaner and holds paint much more readily that hot-rolled sheet. In situations where you aren't doing a great deal of shaping the aluminum-killed sheet may not be truly necessary. But for more typical sheet metal fabrication projects the trouble of finding this specialized sheet is probably justified by the additional ease with which most objects can be formed.

Most common fabrication projects start with sheet steel that is between sixteen and twenty gauge. Twenty gauge is the lightest sheet steel most shops use for any fabricating projects, and eighteen is more common. Sixteen gauge is nice and strong, it's twice as thick as

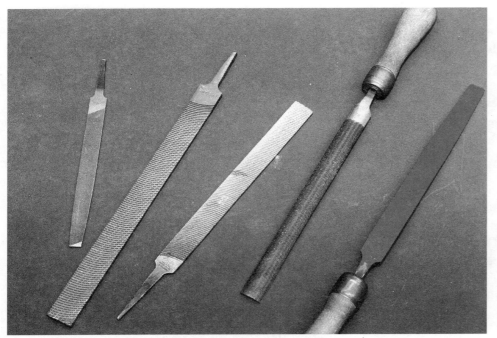

*A few files, both coarse and fine, are nearly essential for any serious sheet metal work.*

the lighter twenty gauge and also at least twice as difficult to shape. Twenty gauge is what most automobile fenders and hoods are made from today. Sixteen, and sometimes eighteen gauge, is what real cars and trucks were made from in the days when Elvis Presley music was recorded on 45 RPM records.

If you take your micrometer to the metals-yard and use it to squeeze a variety of sheets remember the following scale: 20 gauge measures .035inches, eighteen is equal to .045inches, and sixteen gauge steel will show a reading of .063inches.

**Aluminum**

Aluminum is generally referred to by its dimension, and not by the gauge. Common sheet dimensions include .050inches and .062inches. As Bob Monroe points out, "The .040 is really light and it shapes easily, but it's also easy to file through it when you do the finishing." For that reason many of the projects seen in this book are made from .062inch aluminum, sometimes .050. The heavier aluminum has the added advantage of being more durable in day to day use.

Different alloys have different properties. Aluminum rated 6061 is good for billets that are later machined into wheels or hub assemblies. For the sheet metal work described in this book the "pure" aluminum alloys like the 1100 series, or perhaps the 3000 series, are much better. As you will notice throughout the book 3003 is a common sheet alloy used for fabrication projects. The code at the end of the number, like the T-6 following the 6061, describes the heat treatment.

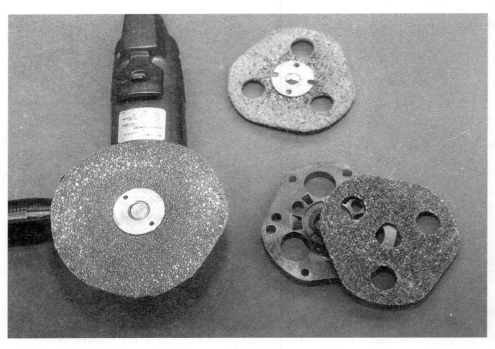

*A small grinder can be used to dress and finish sheet metal shapes and seams. On the right, special Scotch-Brite sanding pads are available that are less aggressive and create less heat.*

H14 is a common designation for a 3003 alloy and is often described as "half hard." It's enough of a heat treatment to give the metal some strength when used on a large panel.

Illustrated farther along in the book is the process of annealing. Annealing returns a heat-treated piece of aluminum to a "dead soft" condition. Annealing can be used to remove the heat treating from part of the sheet, the part that must be shaped. It can also be used as a way to eliminate the work-hardening that occurs as you hammer and beat on a piece of aluminum.

### INTERVIEW: LOREN RICHARDS

*Loren Richards might be called a student of the metal crafting arts. Though he spends his days running a large mold-making operation he spends night and week-ends making special tooling for men like Steve Davis and Cass Nawrocki, and assembling a massive library of books and materials on metal shaping. His position as senior-student gives Loren a unique perspective on this whole business of metal shaping.*

*Loren, tell me a little bit about how you got interested in metal shaping?*

Well, when I was 13-years-old I got my first car, which I built into a custom. It was a '50 Ford in about 1955. I was always interested in body work from the standpoint of building custom cars. About 25 years ago I got interested in just doing the metal shaping. I approached it as an amateur because I have a full-time job. Looking at it as an amateur is a lot of fun.

*But you have a certain expertise because of your background in tooling?*

Yes. I worked as a die maker at one time, a mold maker in a machine shop. So I understood the making of tooling, the shaping of metal, and what can be done with stamping dies.

*When I saw Steve Davis he said that you make some of the tooling for his power hammer, and that you're probably one of*

*This English wheel from Ron Covell has a 44inch throat and a forged upper wheel. Available either complete or in kit form.*

*Having a variety of anvil wheels makes an English wheel more versatile. The English wheel from Ron Covell comes with 6 anvil wheels, one flat and the others with various amounts of crown. All are made from 4143 steel.*

19

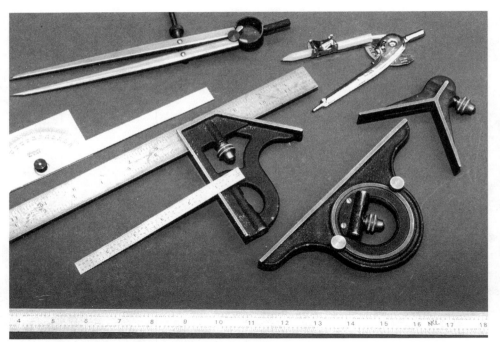

*Accurate measurements and scribe lines will ensure accurate cuts. At the very least you need a good metal ruler and a square, and possibly a compass and divider.*

*A bead rolling machine can be used to create a vast number of different beads and shapes with the right upper and lower rollers.*

*the only people in the country who can do that. How much of that do you do?*

I do it as a hobby, I just make parts and tooling for people I know, friends and such. That keeps me pretty busy.

*You're a big fan of the English wheel, especially for people getting started in metal shaping. Can you run me through what you see as the advantages of the wheel and why you think it's such a good tool for amateur fabricators?*

Car bodies have been built with a mallet and a tree stump, or a body hammer and a steel dolly. If you can weld the panels together you can build some beautiful cars, but it's going to take you a long time. The reason I think a wheel is easier to use for an amateur is that, number one, they're a lot cheaper and you can get into one fast.

Power hammers are noisy, they're big, they're expensive, and the tooling on them is kind of fussy. I think with the English wheel you can do anything that you want to do and do it very, very well. People build just absolutely gorgeous things using an English wheel. I think it's better because you can get into it easier, and you can get out of trouble a little easier too.

*People always think of the wheel as the ideal tool to make a slightly crowned panel. What's the full range of the English wheel?*

The wheel is only used for stretching. You cannot do shrinking on a wheel, whereas a power hammer will do both shrinking and stretching. So that's the biggest disadvantage of the wheel. Beyond that you can make about any panel that you want to make if it's within the size that you can handle. I've heard of people doing 12 foot long pieces for aircraft, you've just got to get a couple of people on it.

*But you can do tight curves then? You can do more than just the lightly crowned panel?*

Yes. Because what happens is most of the time when you're doing tight curves, what you do is just kind of bend it a different way and it opens up that curve. Then you wheel it, and then you bring it back into being a tight curve. Such as if you were doing a fender. The edge of a fender, rather than rolling it where it was all together as a fender, you might just kind of roll it up in a ball, in a tube, and then that flattens the corner radiuses out. And then you wheel them like that so you can get at about anything.

*How big an English wheel do I need at home and how many anvil wheels does a person need to start?*

You could get by with one that had about a 30 inch throat, and you could probably get by with three anvils.

*Do the anvil wheels need to be hardened and/or polished?*

Not for an amateur. You can do a lot of work with a soft wheel especially if you're doing aluminum. If you think you're going to roll over welds though, on steel, it's going to mark-up the wheels unless they're hardened. So I've used them both soft and at 30 Rockwell, and now I've got anvils that are at about 55 Rockwell. You would have a hard time wearing out a wheel. Let's put it that way.

*The wheel transfers its finish to the material you're working on? So a polished wheel leaves the metal in better condition?*

Yeah. It leaves it shiny, but you normally don't care. Because the first thing you're going to do before you paint it is sand it anyway. So that's just a little bit of showmanship, though it gives you nice reflections so you can

A TIG welder can cost three or four thousand dollars, though smaller units are available for about half that. Whether you need one depends on both your budget and the amount of sheet metal work you intend to do.

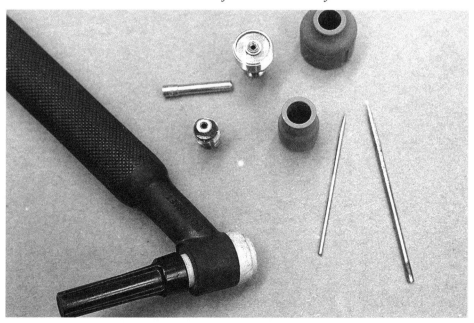

Larger and smaller tungstens are commonly used to weld different materials. Aluminum commonly needs a larger diameter tungsten because it requires more heat than steel of a similar gauge. A larger diameter gas lens like that on top can be used to concentrate more of the inert gas around the area being welded.

*A power hammer like this Yoder in the shop of Steve Davis can be used to shrink or stretch, though it's huge and very noisy.*

*A variety of dies are used with the Yoder, everything from mildly crowned stretching dies on the left to the shrinking dies seen on the far right.*

see flatness and such. It does polish steel or aluminum if you have a high polished roller.

*How about some good beginning project for somebody trying to figure out how to use an English wheel?*

Panels with more curve are easier to do than big flat panels. You can always make a lot of curve in anything. I make what's called dog dishes. Everything that I throw away, I call it a dog dish. I think that kind of works. You just do whatever you feel like. Try anything. Make furniture. Make pedal cars. Do anything. Just start molding metal. The guys that have the most fun, and have the easiest time with it, are airplane guys. There are only a few panels that are shaped. Those are nice to work on. An airplane guy can do his own airplane pretty readily, because their pieces are smaller and there aren't as many to do.

*You said one time that the hardest part of fabricating is deciding where to start on a particular piece of metal that's going to turn into a fender or whatever. Can you explain a little more what you meant by that and the best way around the dilemma?*

There are three phases of metal shaping. The first phase is learning how to make the metal do what you want it to do. The second phase is to learn what you want to do. That consists of really just the observation, and knowing the limitations of what you can do, or what your equipment does. The third part of metal shaping is the artistic part. That's the guy with the good eye that can make panels. I don't care how simple they are, make them look like they belong.

There's a lot more of the eyeball than you think. I'm at kind of the stage where I can pretty much make the metal do what I want it to do, but my big struggle is knowing what to do. The nice thing about working with this is you can keep making them in small pieces. You can start out with a bigger piece, and if you screw it up as you go along you keep trimming it down and saving what you need. It just means you have to weld things together.

I think that the easiest way of learning what a panel does is to take and cut paper and form it to the panel, like a deck lid. Tape it up so that when you get done you've got a complete taped-up piece of paper that looks like the metal it represents. Then you flatten that out. Lay it out on the floor. Get it down flush. See how much crown is in it and work from that. You can actually use that quite a bit as a template just to get you close. With a wheel you have to remember you can only stretch, so any shrinking you do you have to do by hand. You have to figure out where you can make pieces that you can handle and stretch. You better learn how to weld, because you're going to be doing a lot of welding.

*Even though we've talked about the wheel, is it true that you can do a lot of shaping without any tools?*

Most of the time when you talk about a guy doing metal shaping you mean English wheel or power hammer, air hammer, or whatever. Really, for many years it was all done by hand. You can look back at the armor that people did and the silver-smithing. It's all hand work. I think if a guy just started this when you're doing patch panels or something, just forming the metal with hand tools and bending it over the end of a bench and such you could do an awful lot. I think people get hung up too much on having a wheel, or a hammer or such, without really learning what they're doing and learning how to do it by hand.

If you look at the inside of a Ferrari door or something, you can see the way they did a door skin would be to take a piece of flat metal, lay it on a steel plate, take a big hammer and whack it about every three inches across the panel. When they got done with it they had a crowned panel. They did those with virtually no tooling.

*Is it better to start working without a hammer or wheel so you actually learn more about how the metal moves?*

I think the best approach would be to start by hand with a stump and a mallet, and a slap hammer and a dolly, and start making your pieces. Start learning what the metal will do. You'll have surprising success. Most of the people I know who are metal shapers were metal shapers before they got a hammer or before they got a wheel. They were doing it by hand. That's how they started out.

*Any final words of wisdom, besides what you've already said, that you'd pass along to a beginner?*

Right now there is more information available in the tapes and books than ever before, and that is really pretty helpful. That will explain an awful lot. I think if you were to just start shaping, and maybe had somebody who could answer questions for you once in a while, you could get going pretty good. Just get out there and do it. Put in some patch panels, repair a fender, take some dents out of a fender or something.

*An English wheel stretches the metal as it's rolled between the two wheels. The amount of crown the wheel creates can be altered by changing the shape of the lower wheel and by increasing or decreasing the amount of tension (the squeeze) on the metal.*

# Chapter Three

# Sheet Metal Welding

## More than one piece

As discussed elsewhere in this book, anything larger than a simple air cleaner or cover requires the use of more than one piece of sheet metal. Most of your real-world projects will be made from two or more pieces of steel or aluminum. These sheet metal projects might be labeled, "some welding required."

Some say that welding is welding. Yet most experienced fabricators feel that welding sheet metal requires a sensitive touch. Without that touch you

*Most sheet metal fabrication projects involve welding, which requires just a bit more than basic welding skills.*

*The tungsten used to weld sheet steel should be sharpened to a point, with any swirl marks spiraling to the tip. If you don't have a large belt sander, a small grinder/sander like this one can be used to sharpen the tungsten.*

and fabricator. The sequences cover heli-arc and gas welding of both steel and aluminum, followed by a short interview with Neal.

## TIG, OR HELI-ARC, WELDING
### Steel

Neal starts by shearing two long pieces of 20 gauge mild steel and adds a warning. "The fit needs to be really good, each edge needs to be a good match with the other edge. These are sheared, so it's not too tough. No matter how you do it though, the edges must meet."

The TIG welder is set at 85 amps and Neal uses a 1/16 inch tungsten.

"You want to point the tungsten into the center of the joint," explains Neal. "So you heat both pieces equally. The tungsten should be as close to the material as possible without touching. For tack welds I give the pedal a quick on-off burst, that should give you enough heat to melt the material. Go at least half way down with the pedal. This is easiest to do without a rod. To fuse the material like this you don't need as much heat. These tack welds are somewhat brittle, but you don't have to do a lot of manipulating of the part. And doing it without

may ruin those parts you spent so much time fabricating on the English wheel or with a hammer working over a bag of shot.

The intent here is not to teach you how to weld. The book stores and the catalog from Motorbooks are already filled with good books on welding. The idea, instead, is to help you do a better job of welding sheet metal.

The information is presented as a series of demonstrations done by Neal Letourneau, a certified welder with experience both as a high-tech commercial welder and also as a street rod builder

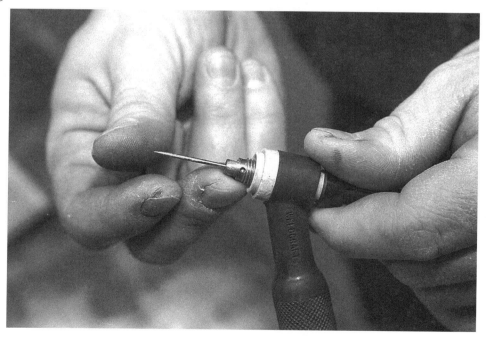

*For welding light steel sheets, Neal equips the TIG, or heli-arc, with a tungsten that is 1/16th inch in diameter.*

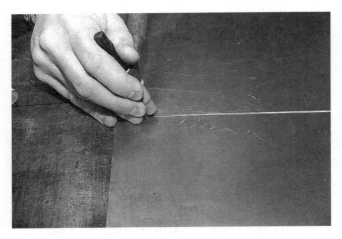

*The tungsten should be pointed into the weld and held as close as possible to the material without actually touching.*

*Neal does the tack welds without any filler rod. Because these fusion welds don't create much heat, the two sheets of steel stay nice and flat.*

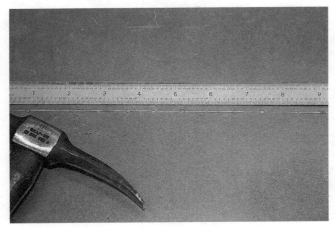

*Neal stitches the two pieces together with tack welds spaced less than an inch apart.*

any filler rod gives you another free hand to hold the material."

Because we are welding flat sheets there isn't much need to hammer and dolly the tack welds. If the sheets do slip during the process of welding Neal puts the dolly behind the seam and hammers lightly from the top to get the two pieces level. If the tack cracks during hammer and dollying Neal just gets the metal even again and re-burns the tack weld.

Once the two pieces are tack welded together we can actually weld this thing together. Like a number or experienced welders Neal uses light wire meant for a MIG (or wire-feed) welding as his filler rod.

"Trying to weld .035 inch thick material with a filler rod that's .060 inches thick doesn't make a lot of sense," says Neal. "The base material will be gone long before the rod gets hot enough to melt. Most of the time I use .030inch rod on 18 and 20 gauge sheet metal. Some people like Ox-weld 65, I usually use 70S-6. Really, you don't use very much of the filler material."

Now we "connect the dots." Neal runs a bead between each of the tack welds, stopping to hammer and dolly each bead while it's still hot, before going on to the next one. The hammer and dolly work is done with the flat side of the dolly and a flat-faced hammer. "We don't want to overwork the metal at this point," adds Neal. "Because it's hot it will stretch. We just want to return the material to a flat state."

Rather than welding in a straight line, Neal welds one small section and then moves down and welds another area in the middle of panel so he doesn't concentrate too much heat in one area. Neal often feels the metal with his gloved hand as a way to judge the heat. "Because we're using low current we've got less heat," explains Neal. "The heat-affected area is pretty small which is good. With a seam that's out in the middle of a big flat piece you need to be careful. If it sucks in you're going to have trouble hammer and dollying out there. A curved piece is more resistant to moving around because the shape gives it strength, but it's also harder to hammer and dolly."

Rather than use a conventional "rod" Neal uses wire designed for a MIG or wire-feed welder. This roll is ER70S-6 and the wire measures .030inches in diameter.

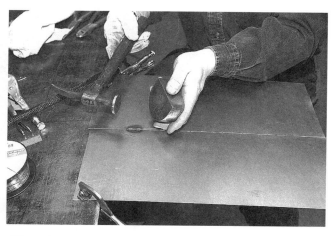

These sheets require matching hammer and dolly with flat faces. The idea is to get the area flat again without causing distortion or stretching of the metal.

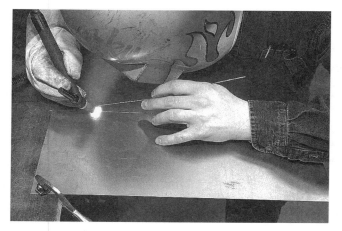

After the tack welds are finished and the two pieces are still in good alignment, Neal starts to connect the dots, welding between tack welds.

The next section to be welded is in the middle of the sheet, so all the heat isn't concentrated in one area. Neal hammers and dollys as needed after each welding sequence.

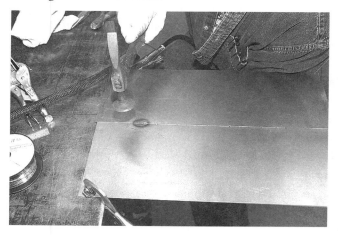

Heli-arc welds on mild steel remain relatively soft, making it easy to hammer and dolly the area while the metal is still warm.

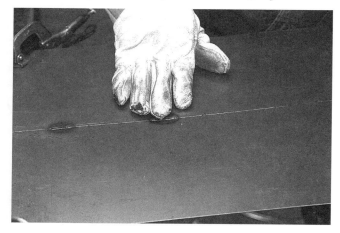

A gloved hand can be used to gauge the total heat content of the metal, and the degree of warpage.

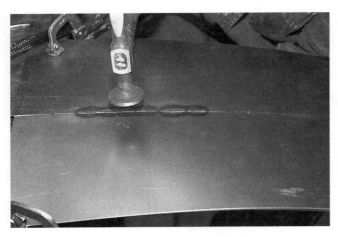

*After each short section is welded, Neal hammers and dollys the area with the dolly held up tight against the bottom of the sheets.*

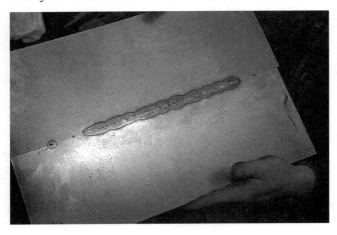

*This is the back side of the welded seam. Note the good penetration which makes for an ultra strong weld.*

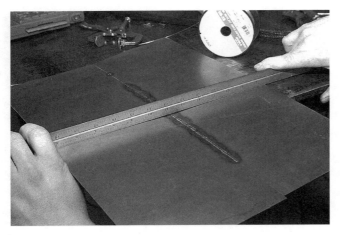

*Here's the nearly finished seam. The TIG welder makes for a smaller heat affected zone and less warpage of the metal than would be the case with a gas welded seam.*

"This is a good example of what can happen when the metal walks apart and then you try to tack it, whoops I blew a hole in it....." admits Neal.

"As you weld the material it changes," notes Neal at the end of this welding sequence. "A flat piece reacts differently from a curved piece. From here you could hammer and dolly this more to get it even flatter, but note the small amount of warpage we've got here."

**Aluminum**

Welding the aluminum requires a different set up for the welder. Aluminum requires a higher setting because it dissipates the heat so fast. Instead of 85 amps, the heli-arc is set at 140 amps. The welder is set on AC, with the high frequency control on "continuous operation."

Welding sheet steel required a small diameter tungsten ground to a fine point. The higher current requirements of aluminum mean you need a larger diameter tungsten, with a ball on the end, all in the interest of carrying a higher current load.

Neal starts by creating a ball on the end of the tungsten. To form a ball, Neal grinds the end of the tungsten flat, then strikes an arc briefly on either the work or the bench. "The end of the tungsten will form a ball almost immediately this way," explains Neal. Unlike steel, you must use filler rod to tack-weld aluminum. The trouble comes from the fact that aluminum goes away so fast during the welding that without a little welding rod all you do is blow holes in the material.

Aluminum tends to move around a lot during the welding, so Neal starts by clamping it thoroughly to the bench. "As always," reminds Neal, "you should have the parts where they need to be in terms of fitment before the welding starts. I space the tack welds 3/4 to one inch apart." Neal adds material to each tack weld, explaining that "otherwise the tack is guaranteed to break, almost every time."

The material is 3003 aluminum sheet, .063inches thick. The filler rod Neal is using is 4043 rod .060inches in diameter.

Welding aluminum definitely requires a certain technique. When Neal pulls the tungsten away from the material too fast after making a tack weld, the material cools so fast that the weld cracks. "Ideally, you want to establish the arc, add material, then back off the heat slowly," explains Neal. "I like to introduce a circular motion around the tack as you let up on the throttle (or foot pedal) to distribute heat and help it cool evenly. If, as you're doing this, you see it's cracking, then you go back on the heat and add filler rod to the tack."

Neal keeps moving the outer clamp down as he adds tack welds. This aluminum doesn't buckle as much as the steel did during the tack-welding phase, though some hammer and dolly work is necessary. The aluminum conducts heat away from the weld more readily than steel, "but where you get in trouble with warpage," says Neal, "is when you go to weld it."

"It's hard to hammer and dolly the aluminum after it's welded," explains Neal. "The best favor you can do yourself is to keep it really flat as you weld. The TIG welded aluminum wants to crack when you hammer and dolly the seam. These are butt welds and they're hard on aluminum because it moves so much. First it rises up, then it tends to go back down, you can watch it happen."

To straighten out a warped seam in aluminum Neal recommends using a dead-blow hammer with a soft face, hammering against the bench or with a dolly held behind the material. Good penetration like we have here makes it hard to get the seam totally flat.

## GAS WELDING
### Steel

Before beginning to gas-weld the steel sheets, Neal repeats what he calls the 100 percent rule: "The parts must fit really well, things always have to be tight."

The basics of gas welding are the same as TIG welding. But with a TIG welder the tungsten is supplying the heat. With gas welding it's the torch that supplies the heat. "The biggest difference between the two," explains Neal, "is the larger heat-affected-zone created by gas welding. It's much more difficult to control how the material reacts because there is so much more heat."

To set up the welder, Neal uses less pressure on both the acetylene and Oxygen than is typically the

*Aluminum moves more during welding than steel does, thus it's important to clamp the two sheets thoroughly to each other and the bench.*

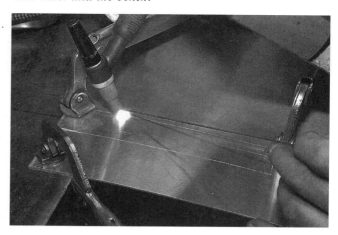

*Filler rod is used to weld aluminum, even for the tack welds.*

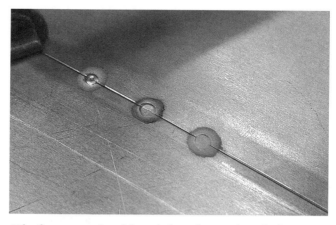

*The first two tack welds cooled too fast, and cracked. Note the crater in the first tack weld (on the left) evidence of rapid shrinking. The filler rod added to the tack weld helps to cool the weld.*

29

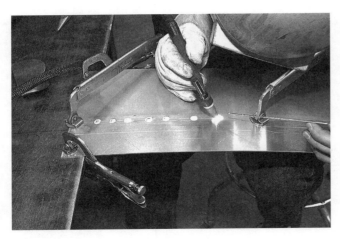

The tack welds are made as a series, the clamp is moved farther out after each tack weld.

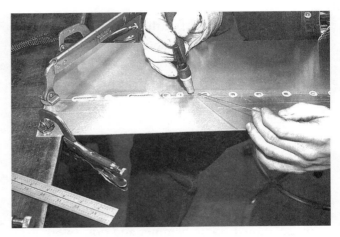

Once the two pieces of aluminum are tack welded together, Neal welds each area between the tack welds. If the tip actually touches the aluminum it must be removed and cleaned.

Even though the welds are fairly brittle, Neal does some hammer and dolly work to keep the two plates even. Once the weld is finished it will be almost impossible to effectively use the hammer and dolly.

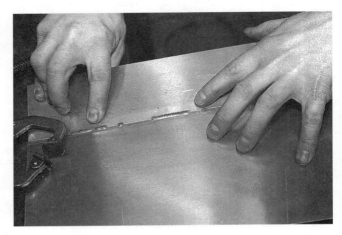

Before going too far Neal flips over the piece to check the penetration. As you can see, the welds have penetrated all the way through to the back side of the seam.

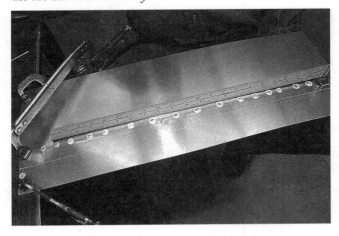

These tack welds are about one inch apart, "more is probably better," advises Neal.

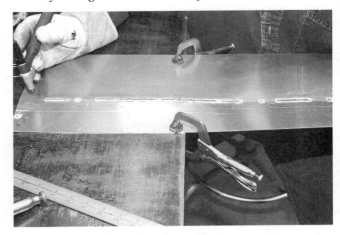

Happy with the alignment of the two plates, Neal continues "connecting the dots," once again welding first on one end and then in the middle.

case for general-purpose welding and cutting. The Acetylene is set at 3psi and Oxygen to 5psi, the tip used is a number 0. "You can always bump up the pressures if you need to," says Neal. The rod used here is Ox-weld 65, 1/16inch diameter. As a rule of thumb Neal likes to use rod that is the same thickness, or slightly larger, than the material he is welding. The material is 18 gauge mild steel, which means the steel measures .047 while the rods measure .0625 inches thick.

Neal spaces his tack welds one inch apart. "In this situation you must use rod for tack welds," explains Neal. "You need to get the base material to where it starts to liquefy. Once it's just starting to liquefy add a dab of rod. Back off the torch if it wants to drop through. Learning to control the heat in that situation is critical or you will blow a hole. You need to be right on that edge. I keep the rod close by, but not in the puddle, and then add material as needed."

In order to keep the seam flat Neal uses the hammer and dolly after each tack weld. This seam is harder to keep flat than the one done earlier with the TIG because the gas welding puts so much more heat into the material.

When the heat of welding causes one spot-weld to sink, Neal is quick to react with the hammer and dolly. "When the spot wants to dip, I push up with the dolly underneath Then I work the top side, along the edge of the

*By sliding both sheets up on the bench it's easier to prevent warpage when welding out near the end of the seam.*

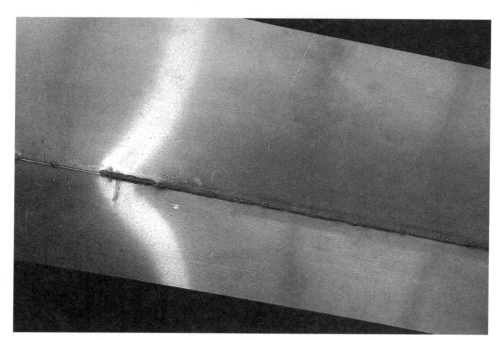

*A carefully aligned seam, a correctly adjusted welder, and the right technique result in a neat seam with minimal warpage and good penetration (this is the back side).*

*Because the seam is brittle a dead-blow hammer must be used if you need to hammer and dolly the seam.*

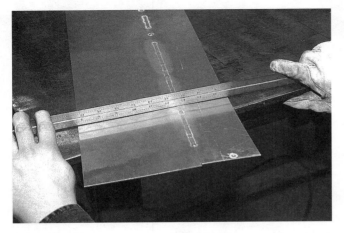

*After a little work with the dead-blow hammer the seam is relatively flat.*

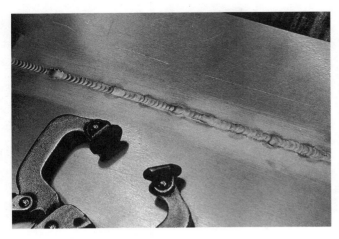

*This is what a good TIG seam looks like on aluminum sheet metal.*

heat affected zone, with the hammer, to bring it back up."

To do the actual welding Neal starts on a tack weld, gets the puddle started and works the tip along the seam in a circular motion. "I move the tip the thickness of the material on either side of the joint. It's important to keep the puddle moving and wet the entire weld area."

Neal "connects the dots" and then hammer and dollies that small seam, and connects the dots again. It's a pretty good idea to skip around a bit to avoid concentrating too much heat in one area. "This will never work as well as a TIG weld," explains Neal. "You have no inert gas to keep it clean, and you're heating too big an area, and you just don't have the same degree of control."

Neal works to keep the material as clean as possible during the welding process, stopping often to wire brush the seam and clean off any scale that develops. When he's all done the seam is neat and reasonably flat, with good penetration through to the other side of the seam.

## GAS WELDING
### Aluminum,

The aluminum sheet being welded in this sequence is more of the 3003 alloy, and measures .063inches thick. To gas weld aluminum a flux must be used to keep the weld area as clean as possible. The flux comes dry. Neal mixes it 3 to 1 with water and then coats the .060inch, 1100 welding rod with the thick paste.

With the same number zero tip on the torch and the pressures set to 3psi acetylene and 5psi maximum on oxygen Neal adjusts the torch to a nice neutral flame. For each tack weld Neal first pre-heats the area to get it molten, and then adds rod material.

"The nice thing about gas-welding aluminum is the fact that the resulting seam is very soft and workable," explains Neal. "This means you can hammer and dolly each of the tack welds in order to keep the seam straight." Once the tack welds are finished Neal cleans the whole thing with a stainless steel wire brush. The next step is to apply flux. Because a good weld will penetrate through to the other side, it's important to apply flux to the back side of the seam if possible.

Before starting to weld Neal pre-heats the area just outside the fluxed area. The flux itself should be dry when you start to weld. "When you see the puddle form, just keep pushing the puddle ahead," is how Neal explains the process. "When it starts to drop though, pull the heat away. You can hammer as you go but it knocks the flux off so you don't really want to do too much hammering."

Neal explains that the technique he uses for gas welding aluminum is different from what he used for gas welding steel. "When you're gas-welding steel you do a circular motion with the tip, but you don't do that with aluminum. Just keep moving down the seam, judge your speed by how fast you're burning into the material. If you set the flame too hot or you're moving too slow you get too big an area hot and burn a big hole. You just need to keep pushing the rod ahead of you."

Because the material is almost dead soft after welding it responds well to some hammer and dolly work. In this case Neal uses a coarse file, the hammer and dolly, and the small grinder equipped with a 50 grit pad to finish the seam. Though it's tempting to use power sanders to finish the seam, Neal warns that too much heat can undo all your careful work. A bit of caution combined with lubricant is a good way to ensure the seam doesn't get too hot.

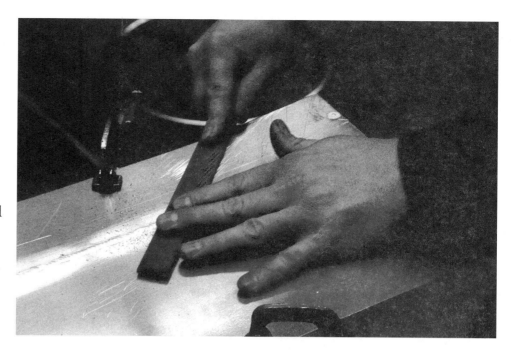

*The 1100 rod leaves a seam that can be filed flat with a coarse file or even a sanding disc.*

*The final results, a nearly flat seam and a strong weld.*

A simple gas-welding outfit can be used to weld either sheet steel or aluminum, though the gas pressures must be set lower than for most other types of welding.

After carefully aligning and clamping the two sheets, Neal begins to place the tack welds. The tip used here is a #0, with a .030inch orifice.

## INTERVIEW: NEAL LETOURNEAU

*Neal, how about some background on you and how you learned your welding skills?*

I worked for Honeywell in their Development and Evaluation lab where I did a lot of work prototyping new parts. No one there really wanted to do the welding, so I picked it up. We did work for the military and for NASA, some of the projects I got involved in were pretty interesting. Honeywell put me through a formal apprenticeship program. Currently I have my AWS certifications for titanium and a whole series of high-tech alloys, Really it all started by going through that apprenticeship program.

I ran my own shop for a while, doing fabrication work. I did lots of stainless and aluminum work. And then I worked for Jim Petrykowski at Metal Fab doing mostly street rod work.

Right now I do my fabrication and street rod work after working my regular job at EPI International. At work I weld up high-temperature, non-ferrous alloys to make components for use in ultra high vacuum chambers, which are part of the semi conductor industry.

*What's different about welding sheet metal as opposed to general welding?*

If you overlay sheet metal joints there's a huge problem later. For that reason, almost every time you address a sheet metal joint you deal with a butt joint. That makes you look at things differently. You have to think about the shape and flatness and how you maintain it when you weld that area. How do you avoid adding too much heat

You're always walking that fine line between good penetration and burn-through. You just can't stay too long in one area. You must be more sensitive because you're right on the edge with sheet metal. The

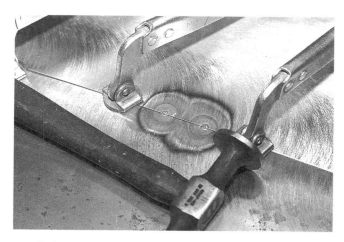

Neal places the tack welds less then one inch apart. Note how much larger the heat affected area is than for a comparable TIG sequence.

Neal does more hammer and dolly work to reduce the amount of warpage.

After doing the first few tack welds Neal hammers and dollys the area to minimize warpage.

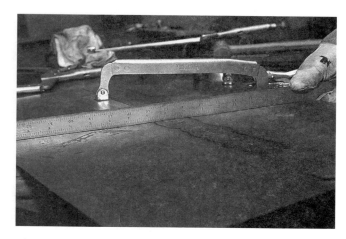

As you can see, the seam is now nearly flat.

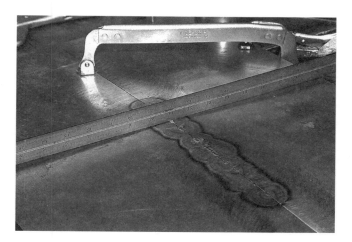

Despite the careful set-up the heat of welding does cause the seam to raise up.

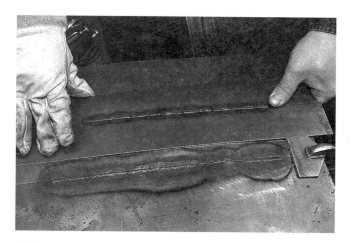

This comparison shows the difference in the bead itself and the heat affected area for a TIG weld (on top), and a gas weld.

Dry powder flux must be mixed with water to form a thick paste. Then the paste is used to coat the rods, and eventually, the area to be welded.

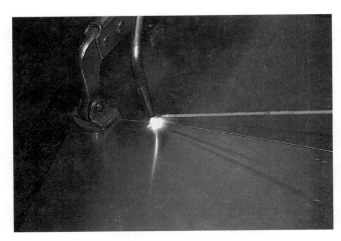

Then the rod, a #1100, .060inches in diameter and already coated with flux, is brought into the flame and added to the area where the aluminum sheet is starting to melt.

To do the tack welds on aluminum with gas, Neal first heats the area with the #0 tip (.030inch orifice) adjusted to a nice neutral flame.

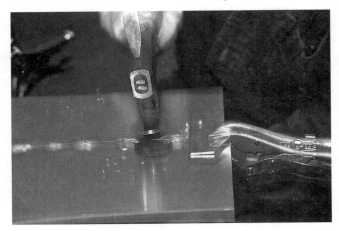

The gas welded aluminum makes for a soft weld, so it's no problem to hammer and dolly each tack weld.

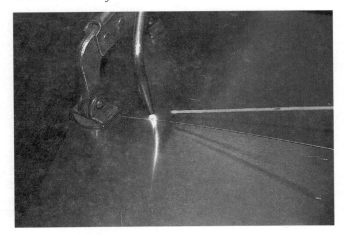

Now the tip is moved closer to the metal until the aluminum just starts to liquefy.

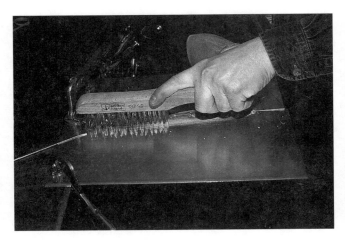

Before beginning the welding Neal cleans the seam with a wire brush. A stainless brush is the only kind that should be used. They do a good job of cleaning and contribute fewer contaminants to the weld area.

thinness of the material makes it important to be on the top of your game, minute changes in current make a big difference, it's not as noticeable with big structural stuff.

*What about the heat affected zone that results from TIG welding as opposed to one left by gas?*

Really, they are the same thing. You are using a heat source to melt the base metals and then adding filler material to replace the alloying components that are burned off during the welding. The difference between the two is the heat source. With a heli-arc, it produces a smaller heat affected zone, an arc is more efficient than a flame when it comes to producing heat, more concentrated.

There is nothing wrong with a torch, however. It's one of those, pay me now or pay me later kinds of deals. You might have to do more finish work with a gas welded seam than you would if you did the same thing with a heli arc.

*What's the key to controlling warpage in steel and aluminum?*

Limit the mount of heat, place tacks 3/4 to 1inch apart. Tack weld, then connect the dots. As you weld the steel, carry the puddle just beyond the second tack, then hammer and dolly that area, just enough to get it straight. Skip around when you do a big panel, like a top insert on a car, so you don't have a big pucker when you go to weld up the last corner.

*What are the primary differences between steel and aluminum from a welding standpoint?*

Steel is a situation where you can use a hammer and dolly on the seam. Aluminum is softer and doesn't respond to the hammer as well. Because of the softness it will get stretched in a hurry, you can ruin a piece of aluminum easily. And TIG welded aluminum does not respond well to the hammer and dolly because it tends to crack.

*What about the hardness of the weld, the workability?*

For aluminum it depends on whether you weld it with heli-arc or gas. If you want the weld area to be workable you almost have to gas weld it. With gas-welded aluminum you can body file it and then run it through the English wheel. A TIG welded aluminum seam is pretty brittle.

It takes time to build proficiency when gas

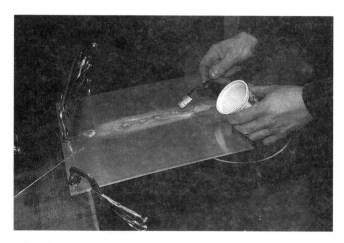

*Flux keeps the seam clean during welding, taking the place of the inert gas used with heli-arc welding.*

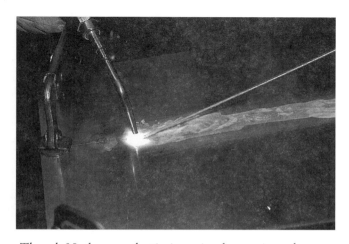

*Though Neal moves the tip in a circular motion when welding steel, he just "pushes the puddle ahead" when welding aluminum.*

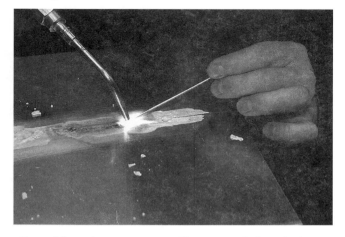

*Gas welding aluminum gives off an orange light, which isn't filtered effectively by the standard welding goggles. Kent White, and others make a special lens that makes it easier to gas weld aluminum.*

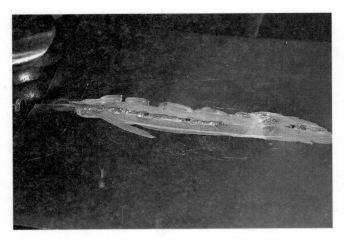

Gas welded aluminum doesn't necessarily make for a pretty weld, but there are certain advantages to gas welding.

After working the seam with the hammer and dolly, Neal starts in on the bead with a coarse file.

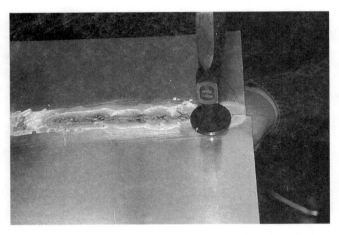

Like the fact that the weld is soft and non-brittle, which means it's no problem to hammer and dolly the seam.

Next comes the small grinder equipped with a 50 grit pad. Lubricant is a good idea here, it's easy to put too much heat into the aluminum with overzealous sanding.

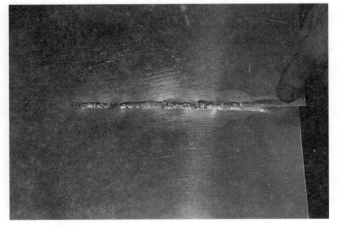

It's important to clean all the flux off the seam with the stainless brush when you're through or the remaining flux will cause corrosion.

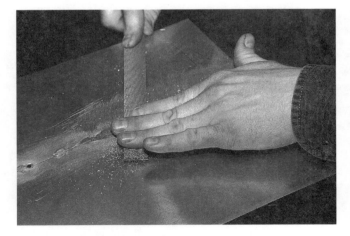

More work with the file will show off the remaining low spots.

welding aluminum, is a skill that takes practice and patience. Aluminum gas welding is ugly. It takes time to make it look good, but if you want the shape-ability afterward that's what you have to do.

When welding steel it's a horse apiece. The softness of the weld is basically the same whether you weld it with gas or heli-arc.

*In terms of technique, where do people get in trouble welding sheet metal?*

When they use the TIG or heli-arc, they set the machine higher than it needs to be set and then rely on the foot pedal to turn it down. Even though you can use the foot pedal to limit the current you should only set the welder as high as it needs to be to get the job done. By setting the machine correctly you can use the full range of the foot pedal. It's more accurate that way. If you set the welder at 80 amps, then all the way down with the pedal is 80 amps. If you set it at 160 amps, and weld at 80, you've got the pedal half way down. You can't back off just a little bit and do it with a high degree of control because the welder is set too high, you're only working with half the pedal's available range. People don't think about it until they start to blow holes.

The other mistake people make when welding sheet metal with a heli-arc is they use too large a tungsten. A smaller tungsten is good for sheet metal, it lights more easily with low current. The arc is established easily because the tungsten heats quickly. For 18 or 20 gauge steel, a 1/16inch tungsten is about right and it should have a point on the end. When you sand it down to a point the swirl marks should swirl down to the tip, like a barber pole, so that's the point where the arc jumps off. You can use a heavier tungsten, like 3/32 inch, for 12 or 14 gauge steel. The bigger size works better in this situation because it takes the heat better.

*What's the biggest overall mistake people make when welding sheet metal?*

They get in a hurry. You have to be willing to be sure that everything is perfect, precise fitment of the parts is very important. Remember that welding is only ten percent of the equation, the rest is fitment, I can't stress that enough. Take your time and don't be afraid to generate scrap. It's how you learn.

*Those low spots can be raised from the other side with the sharp end of the hammer.*

*The work with hammer and dolly, followed by file and sander, leaves a nice flat seam.*

*After welding the two sheets can be formed and bent without any danger of cracking along the area that was just welded.*

## Chapter Four

# Power Hammer Heaven

## Master Craftsman Steve Davis

After more than 25 years of fabricating parts for everything from street rods to custom Harley-Davidsons, Steve Davis has emerged as one of the premier metal crafters in the country. Each craftsman has his or her favorite tool, and for Steve that tool is the Yoder power hammer. Steve isn't put off by the noise or the large chunk of floor space the Yoder occupies in his shop. In the sequence that follows Steve uses his trusty Yoder to form a deck lid.

*They're large and noisy, but for Steve Davis a Yoder Power hammer is the ideal tool for sheet metal fabrication.*

## GETTING STARTED

Steve starts by spraying the sheet metal with a little lubricant, adding as he does, "Everybody has their own secret formula, some people use kerosene thinned with 10-weight oil. I like ATF, half and half with paint thinner or mineral spirits."

Before starting on this little demonstration project Steve adjusts the stroke on the Yoder power hammer. Like a guitar player constantly fine-tuning his Gibson during a performance, Steve adjusts the Yoder again and again throughout the day.

The Yoder is powered by an electric motor with a shaft that connects the motor with the drive crank. The stroke of the hammer is made longer or shorter by adjusting the eccentric at the top of the power hammer. The speed of the blows is controlled with the foot pedal. Note that the upper, or moving hammer, is not connected directly to the drive assembly. Essentially, the upper hammer is connected to the drive mechanism through a flexible linkage. There's enough give in the drive linkage to allow the movable head to continue moving down when the drive crank is at the bottom of its travel. Thus the movable hammer head "slaps" against the lower. How hard the movable hammer slaps the metal depends on the tension in the linkage, the length and speed of the stroke, and the position of the anvil or lower hammer head.

If you look closely you can see that the leaf spring puts tension on the webbing, which allows momentum and the weight of the

*These basic stretching dies used at the beginning of the project have a nearly flat face with very little crown.*

*The dies are held in place by tapered shims. By changing tooling the hammer can shrink as well as stretch.*

tooling to bring the upper tool down on to the metal. The webbing is just the same material used for a power-transmission belt. A special tool is used to compress the leaf spring and disassemble the whole thing so the webbing can be changed or repaired.

For this project Steve starts with a sheet of 3003 H14, half-hard, aluminum .063inches thick. To start the project Steve is using basic stretching dies with a pretty flat shape. The idea

*A partial sample of the dies Steve has collected over the years.*

*Steve starts by spraying his special mix of lubricant on the sheet or 3003 aluminum before the forming begins.*

is to put a mild crown in the metal. Creating a mild crown across the sheet goes rather quickly. Once the crown is established Steve shortens the stroke of the power hammer, with the same tooling, to soften the blows. The idea is to minimize or "planish" the marks left in the metal during the very first phase.

After planishing with the power hammer Steve changes to new tooling: very hard rubber for the upper die and a crowned, metal, lower die. The idea is to begin to roll the edge which will create the lip on the deck lid we are fabricating.

Steve marks the metal where he wants to position the edge of the fold. The mark is made with two scribe lines and a red marker. Then he runs the metal though the power hammer and begins the creation of the flip-up section.

Once he's happy with the initial flip, the tooling is changed to a set of "cross" dies. After each tool change, Steve "test drives" the new tooling on a piece of scrap material. If he's pleased with the way the tooling shapes the metal, Steve slips the deck lid between the tools

upper rubber is the same one we saw earlier, the bottom however has a rounder radius. Steve says, "it's about like a 2-1/2 inch diameter ball cut in half. If it's flatter than this it wants to crown the whole thing, rather than create a radiused, well defined area at the edge of the raised areas. The top of an Oxygen bottle used as a hammer works pretty well here too."

The next step is the creation of a pattern from

*The top eccentric is adjustable, so the stroke can be made longer or shorter, which affects how hard the upper die comes down on the lower.*

and starts on the deck lid again. As Steve explains, "The idea is to avoid hitting it any harder than you have to, so you avoid putting too much texture in the metal. Yet, with the cross dies you have to hit it hard enough to begin moving the metal."

Now Steve changes back to the rubber tool and adds to the flip again, "I don't want to just fold it, I want it to have a certain amount of radius at the point where the edge begins to flip up." Steve often wipes the metal with a rag to keep a light film of lubricant on it "just to help it slide," as he says.

Now another tool change. Back to the cross dies to put more crown in the flip. By working along the edge Steve is able to crown the edge and to add crown to the area just past the radius. Back to the stretching dies. These are used to planish the texture out of the edge. A quick pass through these flat-faced dies and Steve pulls the piece out to check on the progress. Then one more pass through to finish the finish work.

Time to change the tooling again, to create a crown or bulge in the center of the panel. The

*The Yoder has two "ends" with slightly different drive mechanisms. Both drive the upper die through a leaf spring and shackles. Wrapped between the inner ends of the two shackles is the flexible material meant for a power transmission belt.*

43

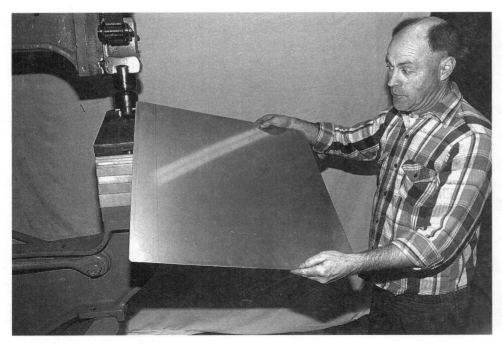

*The "before" picture of the .063inch aluminum sheet.*

*As the upper die cycles up and down, Steve moves the sheet between the dies, following a pre-determined pattern. The idea is to create a mild, even crown over the whole piece.*

light board. Steve then transfers this outline to the metal by scribing the outline and then marking it with a red marker. By scribing a line and then marking the line with a colored marker, the line will always show up, the red marker will never be completely rubbed off.

Now Steve begins to work the area with the power hammer, to create the basic shape. To better define the edge of the raised area Steve works it by hand with a spoon and a hammer.

Now he flips it over and, with a bag of shot placed underneath, uses a soft leather mallet to flatten the area around the edge. The bag in this case is filled with 1/16th inch diameter shot, a mixture of lead and steel. About leather mallets, Steve advises, "they must be very tightly wound, good ones are hard to find. The plastic hammers probably work just as well, and the 'dead blow' hammers work well too. You can grind a little crown on the head and they work great."

After all that work Steve decides that the raised area isn't really nice enough, so he cuts off the top part of the bulge and prepares to make a *really* nice one by hand. Steve can better develop the shape and metal finish the bulge when it's a separate piece.

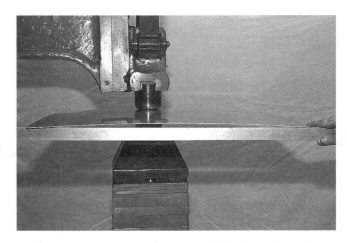

By hammering more in the center of the sheet than the edges, Steve has stretched the middle and crowned the entire piece.

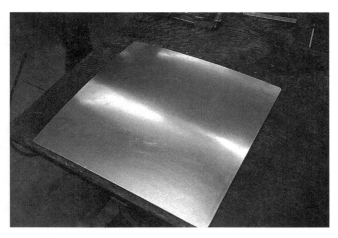

After shaping and planishing, Steve has a mildly crowned piece of sheet aluminum.

Here you can see the hammer marks left by the mildly crowned stretching dies.

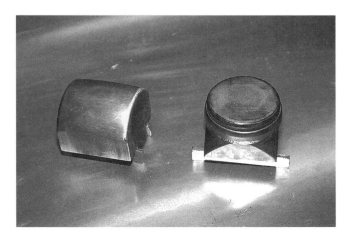

The new tooling consists of a rounded, steel lower and hard-rubber upper die.

Once he has the shape he's after Steve shortens the stroke so the blows have less force, and then re-works the piece. This will eliminate most of the hammer marks left in the surface from the first series of blows.

The line where the "flip" starts is now marked on the sheet with a scribe and marker.

The original template is used to mark out the new cover, though Steve makes it bigger than it really needs to be. He then cuts the blank from another piece of aluminum and files the edge after the cutting is finished. Reference marks are nice and Steve marks the centerline of both the deck lid and the new domed section. He also marks the area that needs to shrink

For this particular job Steve sets up the other half

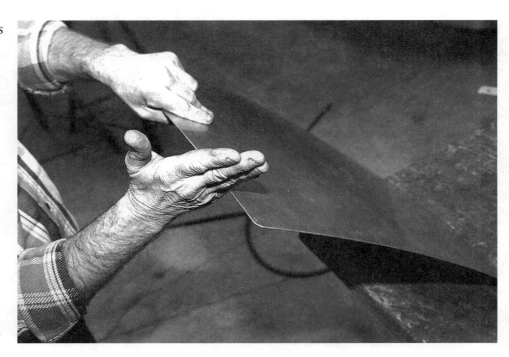

*Steve shows the angle he wants for the edge of the new deck lid.*

of the Yoder, which has a Pettingell head on it that will work better for the shrinking part of the project. "Shrinking is almost always done dry" explains Steve, "you don't want the part moving around."

The shrinking dies used here are the classic shape and gather up the metal quickly. Before the shrinking part of the operation is finished Steve takes a break to stretch the center part of the bulge with a hammer working over a bag of shot. Then he goes back and shrinks the edges more, followed a little more work with the hammer and bag of shot.

Steve made the part too big, explaining, "that way you've got something to grab onto as you work on this thing. When the part is nearly finished he cuts it down to size and finishes it with the planishing hammer. Now he's ready to weld it into place.

This is a good example of how it's often easier to make a complex panel from more than one piece of metal. Before starting in on the fabrication of a panel you have to decide how many pieces it should be made from, how each should

*Here you can see the sheet starting to bend as Steve moves it between the two dies.*

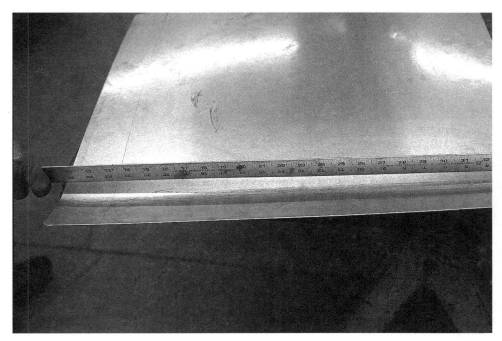

The creation of the flip has flattened the crown in the decklid, a good example of how one step in a forming sequence can eliminate work done earlier.

So you built your own bodies and that's how you started with sheet metal work?

Yeah, that's where the aluminum work started. Everybody could make almost anything they needed. You only bought what was necessary. A few years later I started working in Tom Hanna's shop, in the early 1970s. Hanna was obviously the best body guy around the area at that time.

I stayed there for a year be shaped, and where to best put the seams.

The final operation for this mock-up deck lid is the creation of a 90 degree edge done with a bead roller. "The sharp edge on the upper wheel makes for a sharp turn," explains Steve. "A softer, more radiused upper wheel would make for a rounder corner." Each pass through the bead roller, and Steve makes several, adds to the angle until the turn is 90 degrees.

## INTERVIEW: STEVE DAVIS

*Steve, can we move through some of your early years and where you got some of your first experience shaping metal. Who were the men who helped and inspired you?*

I started working at a body shop in Gardena, California when I was still in high school, just doing straight body and fender work, real simple stuff. It wasn't an upper-end body shop. It was just basic crash repair and enamel paint jobs. I did a little of that stuff there. Then I started building my own dragsters basically, and that's when I had to figure out how to shape some kind of body panels.

These are the cross dies used to put the crown back into the decklid and to add a mild crown to the edge itself. These "hit an oval area about 3/8 by 1inch," explains Steve, "and tend to spread the metal."

*Here you see Steve use the cross dies to put some crown in the edge of the flipped area.*

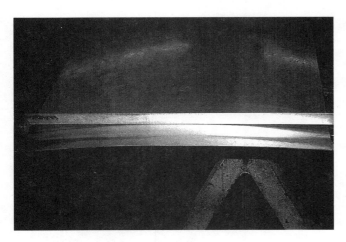

*Patience and persistence pay off. Note the crown in the decklid where it meets the radius, and in the raised area as well.*

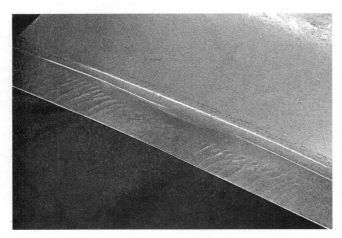

*Shown here is the contact pattern made by the cross dies - more oval than round.*

and a half or so. I picked up a tremendous amount of information and style. Most of that stuff, if it doesn't look good it doesn't matter whether it works or not. Anybody can make it work. I left Tom's to go out on my own. I've kind of been there ever since. I regret it a little bit. I wish I would have traveled around a little bit more and seen a little wider scope of work, because I just got this little tunnel vision deal on how I like to do things and what looks good. I've been fortunate over the years to get hooked up with Arvid "Red" Tweit and some other people that have guided me along with information. But a lot of it, you've almost got to see it done and then go home and try to duplicate it. Pick up the tools you need. There's nothing like experience.

*You said one time that all metal shaping is either stretching or shrinking. Do you want to just talk about that a little bit?*

Stretching, shrinking and forming. Forming is just basically something where you roll it over a pipe or your leg. To get the shape into the piece it needs to be stretched or shrunk, depending on how you want to do it. You can either stretch it up or shrink the edge down. You get the same from both areas. The difference between shape and form, because a lot of that stuff especially big fender style parts that have a lot of tight radiuses, obviously you can't get the tools in so you can take that thing, before you piece it all together and unroll them. It still has the same shape, but now the radiuses are a lot bigger and you can feed them through the hammer. Then you can smooth the stuff out and then roll the thing back up again. It's difficult to explain.

I think the easiest way is the paper pattern deal, where you drape the paper pattern over the buck or part you're trying to duplicate and put the cuts in it or however to get it to lay down on there (see the sequence in Chapter One).

*Loren Richards from Minneapolis said one time that the hardest part of shaping metal is figuring out, with a complex shape, what to do first, how to get started?*

How to approach it is always difficult. Where do the seams go? Do I feel comfortable making that piece or would I be better off to make this one come over there or make this one go up over it. Obviously, you want to make it in the fewest pieces you can get away with. A lot of times on these complex deals you're stuck making them out of a lot of chunks.

*So it's essential to know how to weld? Do you want to talk about welding a little bit?*

Sooner or later you're going to have to hook it together. I think there's a lot to be said for gas welding aluminum panels and being able to work with them afterwards. I know a lot of people feel very uncomfortable with it. They tried it and had only fair or poor results with it. They need to approach it in a straight forward way, welding 3003 aluminum material with a regular 1100 rod. You can buy the rod anywhere or you can buy the 1100 spool wire for a Cobramatic MIG welder. Any of the good commercial flux, ABC flux is still available and Kent White has a generic flux that's almost identical to ABC #8 flux. You just need a regular oxyacetylene torch. A lot of people get into trouble gas welding aluminum because they go too slow. Put a 0 or a #1 tip on there. We use a #2 tip on a lot of the panels that are .060inches thick. Get in there and get the thing tacked together and weld almost as fast as you can. The more you fiddle around, the more oxidization you get, the more impurities you're bringing in from the atmosphere. The flux is starting to fail. You've got crap coming out of the oxygen. You've got crap coming out of the acetylene. The longer you

*In order to create more of a flip, Steve changes to the rubber upper die and works the radiused area again.*

*Again, the hard part is to create the flip, or concave section, running across the decklid without loosing the crown in the decklid itself.*

*These cross dies are used to stretch the center of the flipped area and thus restore any crown lost earlier.*

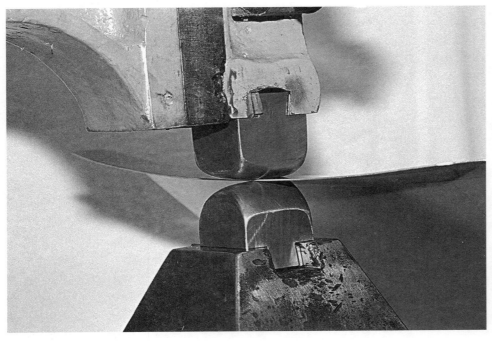

*Close up shows the dies, and the nice curvature being created by stretching in the middle of the raised area.*

stay there the more it's going to oxidize, and once it oxidizes you're pretty much screwed.

*You don't have trouble with aluminum, putting too much heat into the material?*

If it gets too hot it'll just blow a small hole right through it. The more you hang around the more the transfer of heat, which transfers pretty good through aluminum, and it'll start buckling. But a lot of that can be reduced by putting quite a few tacks on the thing. Weld for whatever you feel comfortable with or until you see something start to happen and stop. Let it cool down a little bit. Take a small sandbag or a very, very blunt dolly and just kind of ease those areas up that were going down before you go on. Try to keep control over it.

On the other hand, the heli-arc works wonderful too. On tight corners it works really good using the same 1100 rod and welding it, almost fusing it, together with very little rod. And usually then I'll go back and sear or fuse the backside of the seam together because you don't have the gas back-up on it, and it leaves a pretty ugly weld on the backside. It's almost imperative that you go back and fuse that together, otherwise if you beat on it much the chances of it splitting along there are pretty good. I still kind of like the gas welding just for the romance, and it's an extremely ductile weld. When you're through welding you can put it through any process that you want and feel comfortable beating or hammering on the seam. In a lot of areas you can gas weld corners together. Leave the corner sharper than you really want it and then put a little sandbag behind it with a mallet, and bump that thing back down because it is so soft. The heli-arc welds, even with the 1100 rods, seem to be a little harder because you haven't put as much heat into it. But on all the tight corners and heavier sections and that stuff, the heli-arc - we use it all the time.

*What about steel?*

Everything needs to be at least, at the worst, cold rolled steel. 1018. If you're doing aluminum killed it's all the same process. On all the sheet metal sections we use the regular S-6 style rod. It's a wire-welder rod. It's ER 70 S-6. ER 70 S-2 is just plain old mild steel rod. It's a deoxidized rod, usually triple deoxidized. And the S-6 designation is the softest, the most ductile of all of them. I think it goes from 2 to 6. We use real small rods. On 20 or 18 gauge, we'll use .024 wire which is pretty small wire, and on bigger gaps, no bigger than the .032inch. And it seems like the bigger rods are just a lot of trouble to work with. You get too much of a deposit on each little dip of it. We use the .024 on most everything. Try to put a little spot down and run it an eighth inch or so. Just as cool as possible to where it penetrates through. With a little bit of work, you can get it to where you hardly even need to knock the top off the seam. If there is a

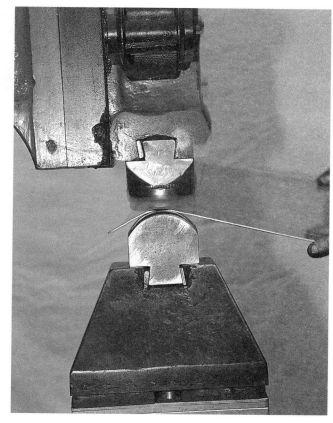

*Now it's back to the rubber upper die and rounded lower, to increase the angle of the flipped section while maintaining a nice smooth radius rather than a sharp bend.*

*Here you can see how Steve moves the piece back and forth through the dies to gently increase alter the angle of the bend.*

build-up on the top, I'll take a cut off wheel on a die grinder, lay it down on a 33 degree angle, and just barely nip the tops off of the weld. And then hammer and dolly it or finish it down. But the S-6 definitely is the rod to use.

For the big structural sections we just use the regular ER 70 S-2, which is old Ox-weld 65. And everybody I know that still builds drag race cars, and everything else,

*A little easy work with the original flat-faced stretching dies will planish, or finish, the surface after all the earlier stretching work.*

*A check with the ruler shows that Steve's been able to increase the angle of the raised area without giving up the crown right at the edge of the radius.*

almost exclusively uses the old Ox-weld 65 or ER 70 for the mild steel and 4130 chrome moly. It gives it kind of an ductile joint. It isn't nearly as brittle. We just have the one rod at the shop, and we use it on everything from tail pipes to funny car roll cages. So you don't have this plethora of rods and get mixed up with this trick deal. Not that there aren't applications for upper-end rods, but if you're going to be putting front ends on race cars, or street rods, or a Harley or any of that stuff, you definitely need to know what the base metal is. If you're un-sure get some professional advice, because there are places where you can get yourself in some real bad spots without working at it.

*Do you want to talk a little bit about the materials? The use for forming sheet steel versus aluminum? Some of the pros and cons? Does it depend on the situation or the person?*

The process is pretty much the same for shaping steel and aluminum. Aluminum is obviously a lot softer to work with. We stick to almost exclusively 3003, half-hard. On some rare occasions we use 5052 H32 which is the common alloy out here. But it's so much harder to work with, and brittle, though some of the airplane guys like it for tanks or they demand it for tanks.

We do most of the aluminum work in 3003. On steel, if you can find it in your area, the aluminum-killed, drawing quality or any of the forming steels are 20% easier to work with than mild steel like 1018. But the processes are all the same. With steel you've just got to be more accurate. Because if you get a blister, or a lump, out in the middle of a steel panel or something like that, you're going to have to go in there and heat shrink it or do some pretty fancy work. Whereas if you get in a little problem with a piece of aluminum like that you can take a little hand shot bag and a mallet and you can kind of force it to do unnatural things. You can make it go back in there. Whereas with steel, once it's out of control it takes a whole lot more manipulation. For the steel parts, with a hammer and dolly, you'd need a little heavier hammer and dolly. Just what we're talking about before - sharper tools. The contact areas would be a little bit smaller. Because on aluminum it's softer so you can contact a bigger area and smooth stuff out.

*By sketching half the bulge and then using that half to create the other, Steve is sure to create an outline that's symmetrical.*

*For reference, it's important to mark the centerline of the piece and of the bulge area.*

53

The upper tooling used to create the bulge is the same hard rubber die seen earlier, matched up to a hard lower die that Steve describes as "about like the top of an Oxygen bottle."

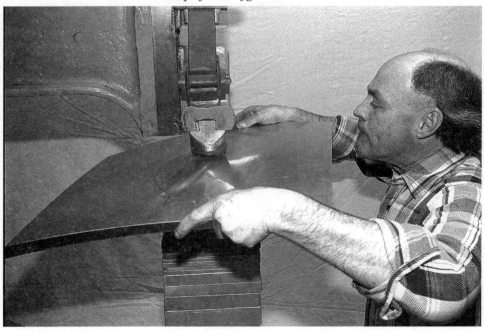

Steve starts out forming the bulge right in the center of the deck lid.

But on steel, because you've still basically got only so much force you can put in there accurately so you need to hit a little bit smaller spots to try to raise it or smooth it. But the process is virtually identical.

*For someone working at home, doing maybe their first small pieces, which is better - aluminum or steel?*

Probably steel because you're going to have a lot less trouble welding it initially. And on steel you can do a real nice job with an oxyacetylene torch. It warps pretty good, but you can produce pretty nice welds that way. If you don't have one yourself, an oxyacetylene torch is pretty easy to come by. Welding is a good skill to have. It takes a little while to pick it up, but if you're going to be doing much car construction it's just going to be critical to have that skill.

*Can we talk about your preferred welding tip size and the rods you like to use?*

With TIG welding I might use a .045inch rod. For gas welding, maybe one a little bigger, because the gas flame wants to ball up the end of the small wires. Just put it in there and try not adding in any more material than you need. A lot of the old Ferraris and English cars, they would fit the panels up so nice. They would just go along with a very small 000 or 00 tip, and just fuse the panels together and use no rod at all. Which you see in a lot of the old cars. It leaves an under-cut weld which you're going to have to fill with plastic or lead or Bondo or something. It works very well, some people call it Scotch-welded. There weren't any lumps to flatten out. They could run it back through the English wheel and it wouldn't stop the wheel at the weld or mark up their wheels. In the very early days the wheels weren't made out of heat treated chrome alloys and these guys didn't want to mark up the wheel. If you put a mark on the wheel every time the wheel goes around it's going to replicate that mark on the car.

*So the welds have to be butt welds?*

Any kind of panel construction is a butt-weld. Overlaps are OK if you're just going to quick and dirty put some patch panels on a car for resale or something. You can get the step pliers and go in there and just spot weld the things and mud over them. It's a perfect application for that. I don't like to do it because you've got this super hard, strong seam. Instead of one layer now you've got two layers of material there - and being able to go back and straighten it out and file it and all that, you're just asking for trouble.

*You do all of your shaping with the power hammer or almost all?*

Yeah, I've used an English wheel a little bit. We did some roof skins for a '32 Ford, and I've dabbled in it, but not much at all. I'm interested in learning the process.

*Because you're familiar with the power hammer can you talk a little bit about the pros and cons of the hammer? Something to pass along to beginners.*

There are not many of them around. They're heavy. They're noisy and nobody wants to be your neighbor. They're hard to come by and they can either be your best friend or your worst enemy. They can be real aggressive and do a lot more damage than good, and the learning curve on them is really slow.

I think probably for a home operation, if you're going to do it, I'd get an English wheel and the sandbag thing because it's quiet and the neighbors will be happy. You can come to the same point just using a different process. Basically, the hammer just goes up and down and compresses the material. The English wheel is the same thing. They both have a small contact

*Steve controls the formation of the domed area by moving the sheet and also with the foot-operated speed control.*

*The angle of the decklid can be changed to further affect the shape of the dome.*

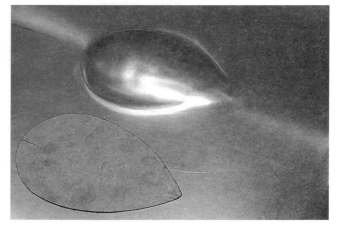

*The basic dome before hand finishing.*

*A spoon and hammer are used to create a better defined edge to the new dome.*

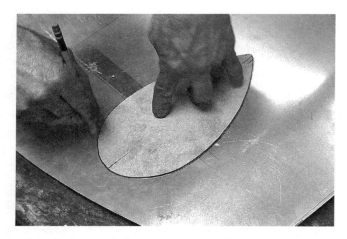

*Though the raised dome is OK, Steve shows us a second way to create the dome, by making it out of a second piece of metal.*

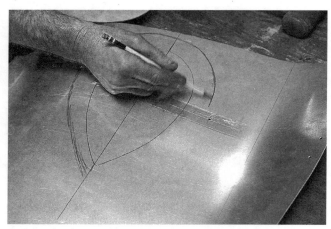

*Here he marks out the edge of the new dome and the areas that will get the maximum amount of shaping.*

point and you roll it through there and it stretches it. Probably the only drawback of a wheel is the fact that it won't shrink, but there are a number of very good after-market shrinkers. There are little Lancaster pump hand-held guys. The next step up would be the Erco kick shrinkers, and then you can go on up into the real expensive Ekhold. It's hard to justify $30,000-$50,000 for the piccolo style machine if you're not going to use it a lot.

Most of the people that do work with the English wheel like Marcel, they'll start the edges down on a big deck lid skin with the big shrinker. They'll shrink the edges down a little bit to get the initial crown into it, and then move to the wheel rather than rolling the whole thing out (check the English Wheel sequence in Chapter Nine). The rolling, to do it accurately, is very tedious. You've got to know your start and stop points. How to get the center up and to gradually work out from there. Basically, the hammer is the same thing. You can go through and manipulate the speed of the hammer and where it hits. You can get it to work less on the edge and more in the center and get kind of a rhythm down.

*You said one time that to get going at home you really don't need very many tools?*

I don't think so. It's amazing what you can do with a handful of hammers and dollies and slappers, and a nice sandbag and a couple of big hammers to stretch the stuff out. There's a lot of really nice cars made with very, very few tools. And there are a lot of really terrible cars that were built in aircraft-style shops. When I worked for Hanna he didn't even have a brake or a shear. Everything was rolled over pipe, cut with hand snips or little electric snips and there was some really, really nice stuff done out there.

With a minimum of tools you may produce more panels to get the job done. You have a few more seams this way. And if you don't feel comfortable welding the stuff together you're going to be in trouble. So, again, it's pretty critical to

The hammer is equipped with shrinking dies. While the other dome was formed by stretching, this one will be made largely by shrinking.

By shrinking the outer edge of the small piece, a dome begins to form.

The outer, marked area, is where Steve will do the shrinking to create the new dome.

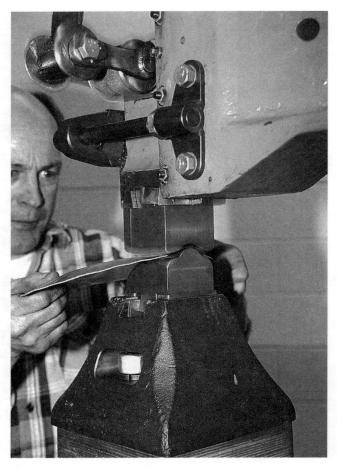

*Here you can see the shrinking die used on the outer lip of the new dome.*

get the welding down. When you get started on some of these projects, they're not going to be a little afternoon six-pack deal. They're going to go on for days or weeks or months at times.

*It goes without saying that patience is a big part of this deal?*

Absolutely. I think you have to start off with a pretty good, realistic plan. Especially if you're just kind of entering into it. Stay away from the exotic. Stay with something that's fairly simple and work your way into it. Start with something like an air cleaner or tank extensions for the back of the Fat Bob tanks on your Harley. Deals like that where you can get your hands around this thing and you're not trying to make the whole gas tank. Take the existing tank and do a little

styling. Do some modifications and do the best you can and sheet the thing with plastic. Those little projects will show you what you can and can't do, where your weak spots and your strong points are, and you can add to your tool collection or change course as need be.

*What's the single biggest or most important lesson for a beginning fabricator to learn? If you could only teach somebody one thing or emphasize one thing what would it be?*

I think it's important that the information you're getting is thoroughly accurate. In the front of the Hilborn fuel injector catalog is a great sentence that says, "Beware of well meaning but uninformed friends." I think there's a lot of hocus pocus out there. Maybe not bad information, but information that is possibly misapplied

*Steve shrinks right up to the edge that was marked earlier.*

and I think when you get started you want to get it out of a reputable book or from somebody that has actually done it. Not one of your friends that heard it from so and so, that saw it done once kind of a deal. I think probably the most important thing is good information of where you're going, what style welding to use for what style materials. What tools to use. I think starting off being very sparing with buying tools. A couple of nice hammers and dollies, and a shot bag. A cap from an acetylene bottle or oxygen bottle is pretty good for raising a lot of metal. Maybe a couple of slappers. Kind of ease into it, rather than going out and buying a thousand-dollar full-journey-man body set. Obviously, if you can hang around with some people who are already doing it, it'll give you some real good insight as

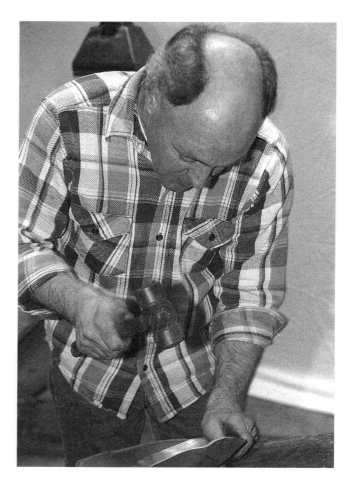

*The stretching part of this operation is done with a time-proven tool.*

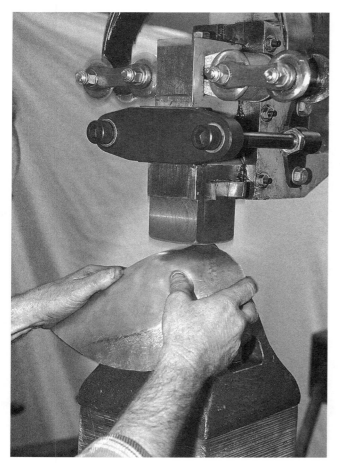

*After the stretching comes more shrinking to raise the dome up higher.*

to what's going on.

*Steve, is there anything that we missed? I'm sure we could talk all day, but anything important?*

Keep it simple. Understand the processes. Don't go overboard on the first deal. Start off with something simple, fill some holes in your fender first. If you're going to do the heat shrinking process, don't start out in the middle of a new door skin on your car. Practice on some scrap before jumping in and doing something dumb. Know the process and plan ahead a little bit. Don't just go in there and cut the top off your car. A little while later you wish you would have moved the saw cut down three inches because it would have saved 150 hours worth of labor if you'd done it that way.

The planishing hammer is kind of a mini-power hammer, designed to minimize the lumps and bumps left by earlier tooling.

After cutting off the old dome, Steve pushes the new one up from underneath and marks the outline.

*You said something earlier today about when things start to go wrong in the middle of a project, don't keep going but stop.*

Yes, when you do something that all of sudden is turning inside out or you're working on one side of the car and the door gap is going nuts, stop and assess what's happening. Because chances are if you go farther it's just going to get worse. It isn't going to fix itself as you go along.

When gaps start to go, or panels start to buckle, something is happening there and you need to really stop and assess the situation. Whether it's re-shimming the body, or cutting a couple of things loose. Because a lot of old hot rods, when you cut a door post loose or cut a panel off, that thing has got tremendous built-in stresses. When everything's holding hands it's fine, but you take one of these strength elements out of it, this thing can buckle or do a parallelogram or doors don't fit anymore. As soon as you cut that thing loose, it's gone somewhere.

Before you can make anymore steps you need to get it back, or maybe even go the other way and over correct for it a little bit. Try to anticipate, because with the sheet metal stretching, no matter how many paper patterns you make and everything else, you still have to kind of anticipate what's going to happen.

I think we talked about body grinders, they're a little overused. I've rarely used a body grinder for anything except for real heavy fabrication construction kind of a deal. I like to use the high speed foam pads with a 40 grit disk on it, where they're very compliant, and just dust over the top of the metal. There's still the big fight over do you prime the car first and put the bondo on later or put the bondo on first and prime over the top of it. Obviously, they both work. I kind of like the bondo over the bare steel, but you argue with the paint companies and the people who do it all the time. With the etching Bondos and that, they're tremendous. They'll last 50 years or better. I don't think you need to go in there with a 24 grit grinder disk and just tooth the whole car up to get the plastic to stick to it.

*You must get a lot of satisfaction from the work you do?*

Well, every once in a while you get on the verge of insanity. The bigger projects go on for 1,500 or 2,000 hours and anybody who says you don't get bored or go mad in the process hasn't done it. I like to intersperse the metal forming with something else. A funny car deal, a little bit of fabrication and chassis work. And I kind of enjoy doing the motorcycle parts because nothing is very big. The biggest part on the whole thing is probably the rear fender or possibly a tank. You seem to be able to move along pretty well on those. But yes, I do take tremendous satisfaction in the work we do here.

*The edges where the two edges meet are trimmed to make a perfect fit and a neat butt weld.*

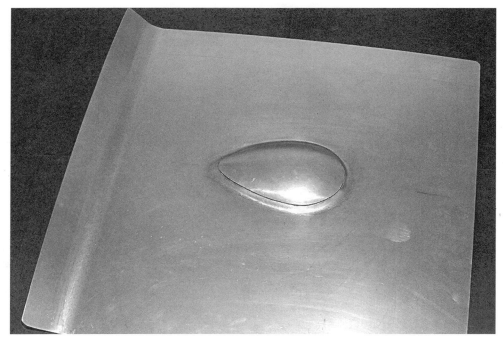

*Before welding, the finished panel.*

## Chapter Five

# Hammerforming

## The Art of Ron Covell

Ron Covell is the man best known as a regular contributor and columnist for *Street Rodder* magazine. For the past 35 years Ron's been bending sheet steel and aluminum to fit street rods and custom motorcycles. In addition to being a generally talent-ed tin-smith, Ron is a big proponent of the ham-merform method of sheet metal shaping. Most of the demonstration work that Ron did for the cam-era involves hammerforming part of a pedal car, a project he already had in the shop.

*This pedal car is the creation of one of Ron's students. For our demonstration project Ron built the back half of another pedal car from the same hammerform.*

The pedal car is the project of Mike Curcio, one of Ron's students. As Ron explains, "This seemed like a fairly good first project, maybe a little tough, but Mike already had experience with wood, which made the first part of the project a little easier."

Before we started on the project Ron explained some of the things he's learned in 35 years of working metal (parts of this are repeated in Chapter One): "There are only five things you can do to metal: stretch it, shrink it, bend it, cut it or weld it (join it). That's pretty much the end of the story. Everything is made through a combination of those processes."

Ron goes on to explain, "...shrinking and stretching, those are the tricky parts of the process. For most people stretching is by far the easiest. You can do it with a hammer, dolly and a sand bag. What drives people nuts is the shrinking part of the equation...".

"The hammerforming method takes the process of shrinking and stretching metal and makes it relatively easy. If you're shrinking with a hammer and dolly, it's hard to control it enough to get good results. If you're working on a hammerform, once you've shaped the form it's a no-brainer to work the metal down against the form. Hammerforming, however, is not ideal for a door skin or top inset, something with a small amount of crown over a large area."

## FORMING THE REAR SECTION OF THE PEDAL CAR

In the case of our pedal-car, the form is already made (more on making forms later), so we can start by cutting a sheet of aluminum to fit. Ron explains that, "The pattern is cut so the edge is just flush with the edge of the form, then when it is hammered down it goes just past the center of the edge radius, which is what we want." The material being used here is 3003 H14, aluminum .0625 inches thick. After cutting the sheet of aluminum to size Ron uses a brake to put a 90 degree bend on the bottom of the body.

Because of the contour near the front of the form, Ron must do some shrinking before he starts working the metal against the hammerform. The metal must be shrunk to follow the contour where

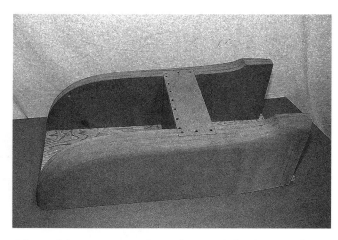

*The pedal car project is formed around this hammerform created in Ron's shop.*

*Ron holds up the first piece of aluminum, cut to match the side of the hammerform. The aluminum used here is half-hard 3003 .063inches thick.*

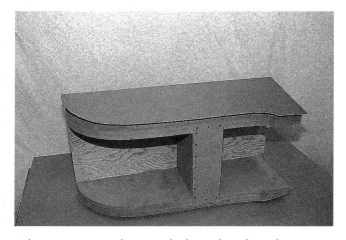

*The piece is cut to be just a little too big along the top where it will meet the center section.*

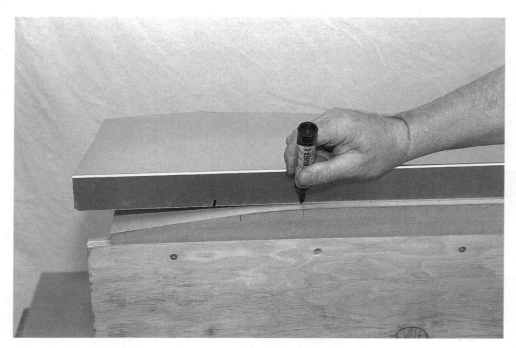

*Here Ron marks the bottom of the side panel where the side turns in. This is the area that he will have to shrink.*

the side of the body becomes more narrow.

The shrinking is done along the edge with the pedal-powered shrinker. Ron stops often to check the fit before going back to do more shrinking. It takes four or five procedures on the shrinker to get the metal to follow the contour of the form.

Next Ron marks the corner where the straight section becomes tangent to the curve. First he marks the form, then he marks the metal. A sanding disc is used as a template and then the corner is cut out with a shears.

The next step is to anneal the edge of the metal. "When I buy this aluminum it's in half-hard condition," explains Ron. "The strength of the material is good, it makes the body more durable and helps keep the panels flat. I don't want to lose the hardened condition for the whole piece, I only want to anneal the places I have to. Also, some warping occurs as a result of the heating, so we want to avoid as much of that as possible. The idea is to make the areas we want to form with hand tools easier to work, and leave the rest of the panel in the hardened condition."

To anneal it Ron starts with a pure acetylene flame and leaves a trail of soot along the edge of the metal. Then he adds oxygen to create a neutral flame, and gets the aluminum just hot enough to burn off the

*Ron uses a foot-powered shrinker to shrink the bottom flange and make the side follow the contours of the hammerform.*

black soot. This is just enough heat to anneal the metal. Then Ron wipes off the remaining soot prior to beginning the work on the metal. Now he places the panel on the form and uses pins to hold it in place, explaining, "These pins are important because they hold everything in alignment as you start hammering." The holes were drilled just after the metal was bent on the brake.

Large C clamps are used to hold the clamping block in place. "I'm just going to start hammering this into place," explains Ron. "There are three areas here: convex, straight and concave, the concave is easiest. I will start on the middle of the edge on the convex part (the curve at the back of the body) and work out toward the edge. When I've got that area close to where I want it I will work down to the other two areas." A slap hammer is used for much of this work because, as Ron says, "it has a large face and covers more real estate than a standard hammer does."

As a measure of how much harder it is to shape the area that is shrunk as opposed to that which is stretched, Ron reports that: "It took 100 hits to do the convex surface, and ten or twelve to do the straight curved area in the middle. The convex area at the back of the body is harder to shape because the metal has to shrink and metal hates to shrink by hammer blows alone. It's easy to make metal bend or stretch by hammering, but if you have to make metal shrink by hammering, you need to set up a special situation. And that's exactly what the hammerform is all about."

The forming goes pretty fast. Ron and Mike plan to build five of these pedal cars, so the hammerform they built is pretty durable.

The form itself is made from MDF, medium density fiber board, 3/4 inch thick. "The reason I prefer it,"

*This close up shows the shrinker jaws. Many shrinkers can also be used to stretch when equipped with a different set of jaws.*

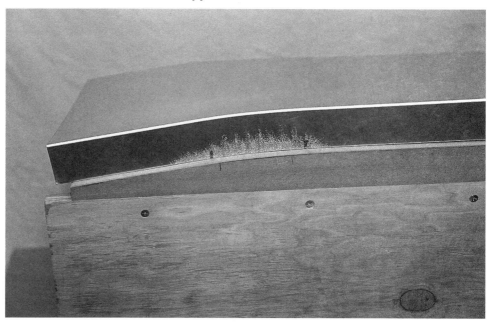

*Here it's easy to see the evidence of the shrinking and how it caused the side to turn in.*

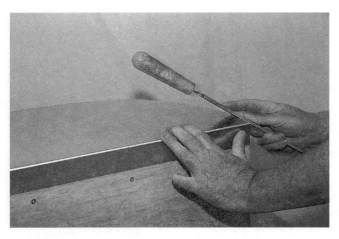

Ron keeps the edges of the sheet filed smooth so they are easier to handle.

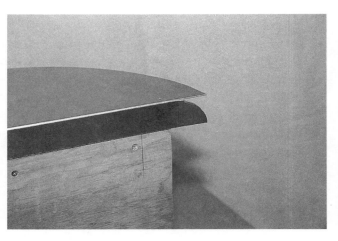

This cut will allow the sheet to bend around the corner.

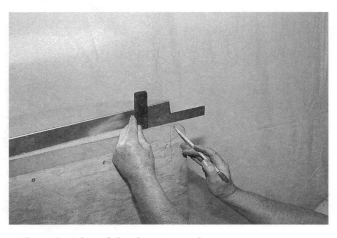

Where the edge of the sheet turns the corner, a recess cut must be made on the bottom edge.

Ron starts the annealing by putting a thick layer of soot on the edge of the aluminum sheet.

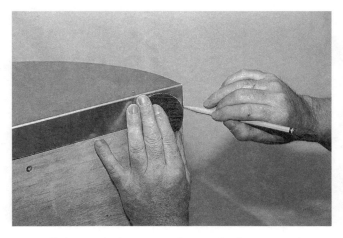

A small disc with the same radius as the form is used as a template.

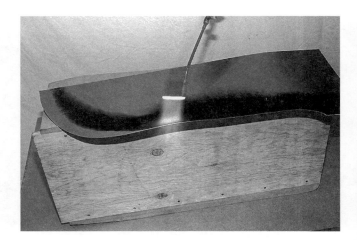

Then, with a neutral flame, he gets the aluminum just hot enough to burn off the soot.

explains Ron, "is that it's much better for this application than particle board. It's a bit softer. Particle board seems rough and abrasive by comparison. It seems to contain too much grit, as if they throw in the sweepings off the floor when they make the material, and it dulls my saw blades. The MDF isn't too hard to find. They often use it as under-layment under Formica counter tops so plenty of lumber yards carry this material."

Back to the shaping. The first step pretty much shaped the metal, but it's still one quarter inch away from the edge in the areas that had to shrink. Ron explains that the metal, "doesn't want to shrink any more than that with the hammer. We need another technique to pull it down tighter."

"We just gently put a few shrinks on the edge," explains Ron. Again, it's a matter of shrink and check, and then shrink some more. After a bit of this additional shrinking the metal is pulled up nice and tight. Now Ron puts the clamping blocks in place again, to address the metal uphill from the edge because it isn't pulled down tight. This work is done with a small hammer with a slightly-crowned head and leaves this piece pretty much done.

Now Ron starts on the other side. The panel is already cut, and Ron drills a hole for the pin, "I put the hole near the edge," explains Ron. "Remember you have to fill these holes later and a hole in the middle of a panel is going to create maximum distortion when it's filled."

The pins Ron uses to hold the sandwich of wood and aluminum together are made from 1/8 inch welding rod. After drilling Ron marks the areas that must be shrunk and cut out.

Ron places both side panels on the form and then measures the decklid. Ron leaves 1/4 inch too much material on the piece he cuts, explaining that, "you might want to leave a bit more than that for something you're forming freehand."

Next Ron starts bending the big radius. Much of the bending is done with the metal clamped into the brake. At this point the brake is just a clamping fixture, the actual bending is done freehand.

If he goes too far, Ron can unbend it in the brake, or, for more precision as to where the unbending occurs, he can unbend it in on the table

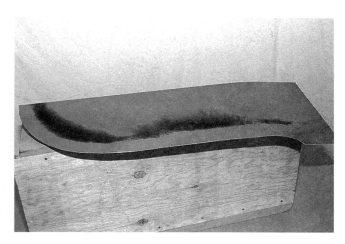

*Here you can see how Ron annealed the entire edge of the sheet, which makes it dead soft and much easier to shape.*

*A clamping block is used to hold the aluminum sheet in place during the forming part of the operation.*

*Made from welding rod, this is one of two alignment pins Ron uses to locate the clamping block.*

*Large C-clamps are used to securely hold the clamping blocks in place.*

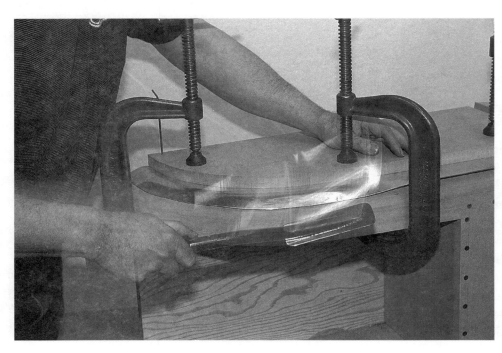

*A slapper, or slap hammer, is used to begin shaping the metal along the curved section at the back of the body.*

- you know exactly where the unbending happens that way.

Once the big radius is formed Ron uses the brake in a conventional fashion to form the flange at the bottom of the panel. "This will unbend the curve in my decklid a little bit," says Ron, "but we can correct for that without any trouble."

Now Ron positions the two side panels on the form. Next he trims the bottom of the deck lid to fit between the side panels and installs two small screws to hold it to the form on the bottom.

Time now to anneal the edge of the deck lid, an act necessitated by the need to shrink the edges over the hammerform. Ron explains that, "It takes fewer hammer blows after it's been annealed, the metal is more friendly. You can quench it in water or allow it to air-cool, the net effect is the same either way."

After punching two small holes for screws near the top edge of the deck lid, Ron screws the deck lid to the hammerform. A tie down strap with ratcheting tensioner is used to ensure the deck lid is held down tight against the contours of the hammerform. Two screws are added to the small holes near the top of the hammerform to hold it in place.

With the panel in position, Ron starts on the edge of it with the slapper tool. When asked how he knows the edge of the deck lid will match up to the edge of the side panels, Ron explains, "On this panel I allowed almost a full quarter inch of extra material along the perimeter when I cut the piece. We will overlap the panels, scribe a line and cut right along the line so the pieces fit exactly."

Once the deck lid and side panels are in place, Ron uses a putty knife to encourage one panel to overlap the other. With everything carefully clamped and positioned, Ron marks the edge where the panels overlap. When it comes time to trim the panels, Ron has definite opinions as to the shears he uses. "For cutting the aluminum, or steel," says Ron, "I like to use Wiss-brand shears. You can buy some that look the same and cost half as much, but they only work about half as well."

Time now to put all the pieces together and then do the tack welding.

Ron explains that if you have to tack weld the panels when they are off the form, (as you would if you were working with a gas-welding outfit) you need to first scribe witness lines on the two pieces before they are removed from the hammer-form. With a heli-arc welder, however, you can tack weld right on the hammerform without damaging the form.

By ensuring that the panels fit precisely together, Ron makes the job of welding, and even tack-welding, much easier. "If the panels fit really nice, then you can just tack the parts together with a series of fusion welds. You could add material with a

*A small body-hammer is used along some areas of the big convex curve.*

*The simple curve at the top of the body, and the concave area, are the simplest to shape.*

69

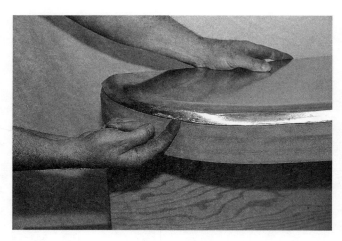

*Along the convex curve it's hard to get the metal to shrink down until it's tight against the hammerform through the use of a hammer alone.*

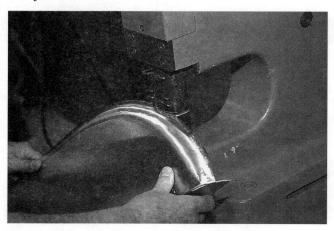

*To make the metal pull in tighter Ron uses the shrinker along the edge...*

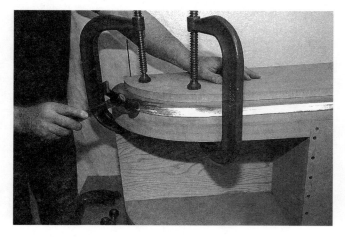

*...followed by a few more well-placed hammer blows.*

rod, but that takes a third hand." In this case Ron uses one hand to hold the two parts snugly together and the other to hold the torch. "I only do fusion welding if I have to use the other hand to hold the parts tightly together, otherwise I do add filler to the weld. You have to remember that fusion-weld tacks are tenuous, not as strong as those made with rod."

After each tack-weld Ron taps the area lightly with the hammer. "I usually start in the middle of the most difficult area and then work out both ways with my tack welds," says Ron. "In this case I started in the middle of the radius and worked outward from there, spacing the tack welds about one inch apart."

When one side is tacked together, Ron flips the hammerform over - placing a blanket on the table so as not to scratch the aluminum - and repeats the process on the other side.

The welding rod that Ron uses is 1100, pure aluminum, 1/16 inch diameter, the same diameter as the thickness of the material.

Ron is quick to point out the tricks he's learned after many years of welding aluminum. "I have some idiosyncrasies about the way I weld aluminum. I use a tungsten that is 3/32 inch diameter, one that's sharply pointed. If you read a welding book they say to use a pure tungsten and put a ball on the end of the point. The concept is good for welding thick aluminum, the ball makes a broader arc and can carry more current. For thin sheet metal, however, I have better control with the sharply pointed tungsten, which focuses the arc into a smaller puddle. Since, in my work, I'm going back and forth between aluminum and steel I find I can use the 2% Thoriated tungsten for both with good success."

The hammerform is now disassembled, it was designed to come apart, then Ron wire brushes the seam and prepares to do the final welding. "Before welding I will go over the seam with the hammer and dolly to make it fit as good as it can," explains Ron. "Sometimes one edge is sticking up higher than another and I want that fixed before I begin welding."

"Actually, the purpose of the hammer and dolly is two-fold: I want the two edges to meet, so one isn't higher than the other. And I also want to get out the worst of the peaks and valleys. The dolly you use should match the contour of the inner radius. If it does it makes your job much easier. Usually the dolly has a smaller radius and then you have to be more accurate about where you put the dolly so it's positioned on the other side of the spot you're hammering."

Because the curved areas have strength due to their shape, warpage isn't much of a problem in this situation. "This aluminum is twice as thick as the steel we might have chosen for this job," adds Ron. "So that helps it absorb more heat without creating any warpage."

Though it might seem like Ron is through with welding on this seam, the next step is to fusion weld the seam from the inside. "I like to hammer the weld flat on both sides," explains Ron, "and with the ridges on the inside of the weld where the molten aluminum came through, it's difficult to hammer it flat. So I fusion weld the inside to flatten out that ridge, then I can go in afterward and hammer and dolly that seam flat."

For sanding the seam Ron likes small, 50 grit discs from 3M on a small air-grinder. At this point the piece is coming along nicely and it's time to finish the seam. Ron sanded off the top of the weld then files it. The file only hits the high spots and thus shows up the

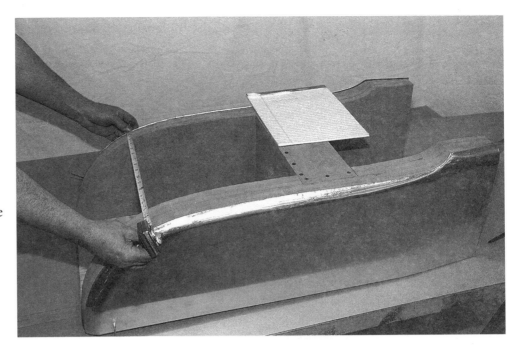

*With the two sides in place Ron can measure and cut the center panel.*

*Though he uses a shear, nearly any cutting tool that leaves a clean precise edge, could be used to cut off the aluminum sheet.*

*Ron uses the brake as a way to clamp the sheet, and begins the process of bending by hand.*

low spots. The idea is to gently raise the low spots before filing again. "You're done when the file touches every surface," says Ron.

Ron starts by running his hand along the seam, knocking down any obvious high spots with the slap hammer. Then he starts with the files. These are both Vixen files, one is flexible. Though you can use soap as lubricant when filing on aluminum, Ron usually does not.

"Because this is .062inch material you don't have to worry much about filing through or making the metal too thin." explains Ron. "I've actually cut some test pieces in half after finishing and measured them. I usually take off .005 to .007inches of material. If it's .050inch aluminum you have to be very, very careful and that's one of the reasons I prefer the .062. Finishing by way of pick and file is easier than the hammer and dolly method for most beginners so the heavier material adds a nice margin of

safety. I would recommend beginners start with .062 inch or heavier material."

After the first round of filing, Ron uses the bulls-eye pick to raise the low spots. The synthetic tip is his own product, designed to be softer than metal. Because the tip is softer it has a little give and doesn't leave much of a mark, especially in aluminum. "I can see the metal move when I hit it," says Ron, "and the hit doesn't have to be very hard."

The finishing process Ron is going through is much like conventional high-quality body work. In that case a light coat of contrasting primer is often sprayed on the body panels near the end of the block sanding process. Further block sanding shows up the low areas as dark spots where the darker primer remains. In this case the low spots generally show up without the need for extra contrast, though Ron explains that, "If an area is really fight-

*Many test fits are required for this part or the job.*

72

ing me I will spray on a coat of Dykem, the bluing material that machinists use, but that makes the area harder to file. You could also use a light coat of dark paint like you would with body work."

At this point the rear body section is essentially finished. Though all these parts could have been formed by another method, the hammerform method means only that the builder have a certain amount of wood-working skill, a small shrinker and a few hammers and dollies. Not only does this process make the shaping part of the operation much easier, it also means Ron and Mike can make 10 or 50 pedal cars from the same hammerform.

## MAKE A HAMMERFORM

To illustrate how hammerforms are built, Ron makes a simple form from his favorite material, 3/4 inch MDF. Ron marks out some nice round shapes and then cuts the MDF on the band saw. After touching up the edges with the sander Ron takes the piece over to the router table.

The router is equipped with a carbide rounding-over bit, used to cut a nice rounded edge. Next we need a clamping block. This is essentially a smaller block that holds the metal flat during the forming process. After creating the clamping block in a size slightly smaller than the form, Ron drills holes for the alignment pins.

The next step is to set the hammerform over the raw piece of metal and drill alignment holes in the metal. To mark the metal, Ron scribes it with a special tool that creates a line 5/8 inch outside the edge of the hammerform. A compass could be used for this as well. The material, 3003, H14, aluminum .050 inches thick, is now cut out on the band saw.

For the actual shaping Ron starts to work the metal with a small hammer.

*...Followed by more careful hand work.*

*When the piece is pretty well formed Ron uses the brake as a brake and bends a flange along the very bottom.*

73

*Time now for another test fit.*

need to overwhelm it."

The corner does come around, in part with help from the dolly used to keep the metal across the corner from bouncing away. "I really am enthusiastic about this process," explains Ron, "because it makes it easy to do things with metal that would otherwise be very difficult."

Ron now repeats the process for the other sharp corner: Heat and hammer, heat and hammer, explaining as he goes that, "if this were steel I would do it the same way, but I would heat the metal until it turned red, or at least blue. And the process would be slower. Aluminum doesn't change color when it gets hot, so you have to be careful that it doesn't melt away on you. I just run the flame over the metal, work it until I feel it doesn't want to move anymore, then heat it again. A person with less experience could just 'soot it up' with

*Before cutting Ron measures for the cutout on the bottom where the two sheets would otherwise overlap.*

As Ron works the material against the form, the corners do not want to shape easily because the material is still in the half-hard condition. "My thinking is that by putting some shape in the part first," explains Ron, "the curve at the edge would hold the center part flat and give it some strength. But I've gone as far as I can here without annealing. It's time to anneal the edges so they will form more easily."

Now it's time to put the aluminum back in the hammerform with the clamping block in place. "The metal is easier to work now," explains Ron, "and lays down readily in areas where all it has to do is stretch. The corners, however, where the metal has to shrink, still don't want to form to the sharp corners. Ron heats and hammers and heats and hammers the corners, and it almost comes around. "We're really making the metal do something it doesn't want to do on that corner," notes Ron. "We

74

Ron anneals the edge of the new center panel in the same way he did the sides.

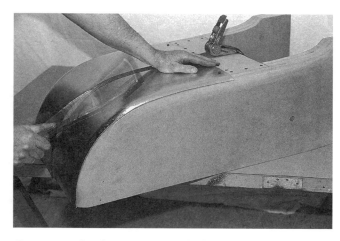

Ron uses a slap hammer to work along the edge of the convex section where the center section meets the side.

Then the panel is clamped onto the hammerform with a cargo strap and ratcheting clamp.

With a putty knife the top or center piece is encouraged to slide over the side panel.

More work with the slap hammer, much like the work that was done to the side panels.

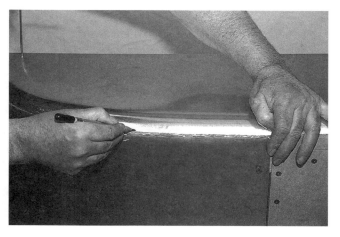

With the two panels held tight against the hammerform, Ron marks the edge where one panel overlaps the other.

*A brand-name aircraft shear is Ron's tool of choice for cutting a neat, accurate edge.*

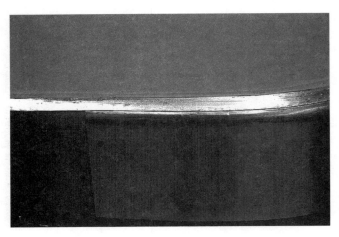

*Here you can see how well the two pieces of aluminum fit before the welding starts.*

*Though the first few tack welds are done with no filler rod, Ron soon changes to tack welds done with the aid of a little filler rod.*

acetylene each time, and then heat it until the soot burns off, that's a real good temperature indicator." At this point the piece is basically done. What looks like a crease is just soot.

Ron uses a Scotch Brite pad to clean the piece up, explaining as he does, "If I were going to polish the part, I would go over the edges with the hammer and dolly and then metal finish all the areas that were shaped so there are no low or high spots."

## WHEEL DEMONSTRATION

Before leaving Ron's shop, he did a short demonstration of the English wheel. "If you think about it, a hammer and dolly compresses the metal between the hammer and the dolly," explains Ron. "The wheel does the same thing, it stretches the metal between the upper and lower wheel, it takes very little effort and leaves almost no tool marks. We sell two English wheels, the big one comes as a kit or as a completed machine. If the buyer assembles the kit, it takes about two days and saves him $1100.00."

How big a wheel does a person need? "We sell a bench top English wheel, 20 inch throat, good for small projects and learning the process. But it only works at 1/4 the speed of a big machine because the contact patch between the wheels is so much larger with the big machine." Ron adds the suggestion that, "It's a good idea to de-burr the edge, for safety, as you know the metal can take on a razor-sharp edge."

For the demonstration project Ron is going to dome a piece of metal that will become part of the cowling for an airplane nose. A buck is used here, and while bucks are used primarily for checking the size and progress of a piece of metal being formed, "in this case the buck encompasses the characteristics of both a buck and a hammerform," explains Ron. "The top is essentially a hammerform, it seemed like a natural to combine the two for this project."

We will use the wheel to form the small piece for the corner of the form. The raw material is cut out of a larger piece of .062inch, 3003 H14, aluminum. Ron starts the forming over his knee, then moves to the wheel to put a compound curve in the metal.

"People get goofed up because steering the metal through the wheels is backwards, almost like

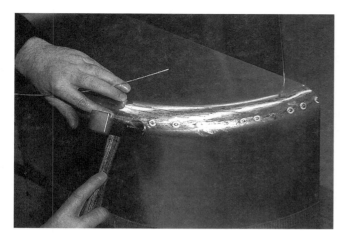

Each tack weld is lightly hammered before going on to the next.

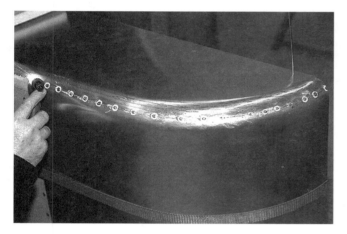

The tack welds are very neat and spaced one inch or less apart.

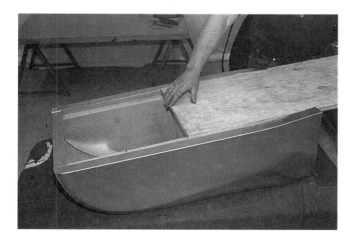

The hammerform is designed to be disassembled and then collapse so Ron can take it out of the body.

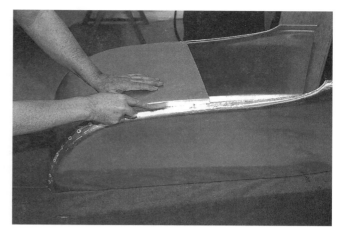

Before doing the final welding, Ron wire brushes the seam to eliminate any material that might contaminate the weld.

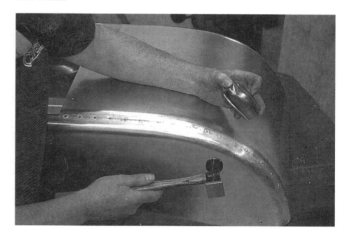

A hammer and dolly, with a shape matching the radius of the inside of the body, is used to knock down any high spots.

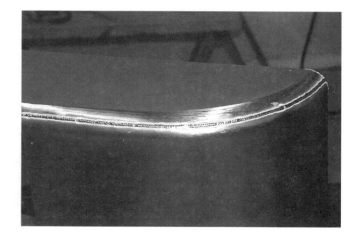

The finished, TIG-welded seam ready for more pick and hammer work and then the finishing.

*This close up shows the inside of the seam, where the ridge left by molten aluminum was eliminated by fusion welding.*

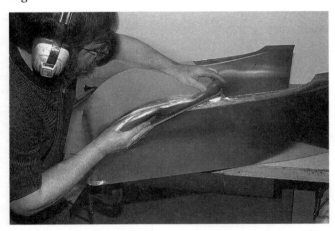

*A Vixen file is used to minimize the high spots and show up the low spots.*

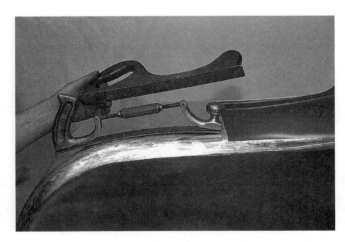

*Here you see two Vixen files, one mounted on a handle that allows it to be arched to match the contour of the object being filed.*

backing up a trailer," explains Ron. "I start with the two wheels spaced apart by about half the thickness of the material. Steel and aluminum work the same, the techniques are the same." It's interesting to note that this piece is not annealed because, as Ron explains, "The wheel generates enough force that you don't have to anneal the piece. People think you have to have lots of pressure between the wheels to make it work, and you really don't, it will shape with as little as 20 pounds of force, and you seldom need more than 100. I often spin the upper wheel just before I slide the metal between the wheels so it's easier to get the metal started."

"Almost everyone pinches their thumb in this machine at least once," warns the operator. "Choose the wheel with the radius closest to what you're trying to achieve, that's why it's nice to have a broad selection of anvil wheels."

The first passes are made at moderate pressure. After the piece has most of its shape, Ron goes over the whole thing with light pressure. This is called "washing over" and evens out the slight variations you get in the metal at moderate pressure.

The contact patch between the wheels for this piece is about 5/16 inch. Ron explains further. "The individual tracks should be parallel and almost touch. The spacing must be even or you will get more curve in one part of the piece than in another." When the piece fits pretty well, Ron changes wheels. The new one has more crown. Ron runs the edges of the sheet through the wheel while leaning on the metal and bending it down as he goes. This puts a nice, sharp, radius all along the edge of the part.

With all the edges "radiused," Ron uses a small shrinker to eliminate the "ruffles" at the sharpest corners, areas where the metal doesn't want to form because it needs to shrink. Now he uses the wheel to blend the area that's been shrunk. And that's the end.

## INTERVIEW: RON COVELL

*Ron, tell me a little bit of your early history and how you got involved in metal shaping?*

I was always fascinated with cars. Even as a pre-teen, I could name every car that was on the road and usually the year and model. It seemed like my overriding interest in cars was not the mechanical part. I had some interest in drive trains and engines, but I was more interested in the body and particularly the styling of the bodies on cars. At a pretty early age I saw a book that showed Italian coach builders making bodies for Ferraris and Maserattis, and they were working literally with wooden mallets, hammering into tree stumps. Those were the primary tools they used, and they created these elegant shapes. We're talking about the mid 1960s Ferraris and Maserattis. I was just fascinated by that. So over the years, I looked for ways to develop talents in that direction. I started by taking an auto body repair class at a local junior college, and I learned quite a bit there. I did my first work with lead in that class. I think I took about three or four semesters. I learned basic hammer and dolly techniques, and how to spread plastic filler and sand it down.

Around that time I learned of a man named Arnie Roberts who worked in the San Jose area, and built dragster bodies and sports racing car bodies. I went to see him and told him I was really interested in learning what he did, and he said I could come to work there part-time if I wanted. I learned a tremendous amount from Arnie Roberts. He discovered pretty quickly that even if he stopped paying me I would continue to work there. So most of my apprenticeship was unpaid, but I learned a tremendous amount from Arnie Roberts. I learned about annealing aluminum and working with a mallet and sandbag, the fine points of hammer and dolly work, aluminum welding - gas welding aluminum. After eighteen months of working with him, I really had mastered the basic set of skills required for metal fabrication.

I think right after that I got a job working for Fiberfab, a company that made kit car bodies. I didn't really work with fiberglass there. I helped put together their prototype cars and their display cars. After about six months of that I got a phone call from Kent Fuller for whom my previous boss, Arnie Roberts, did much of his work building bodies for his dragster chassis. Fuller was looking for someone to build the bodies for his chassis and offered to set aside a corner of his shop, buy a brake and a shear and basically feed me all the

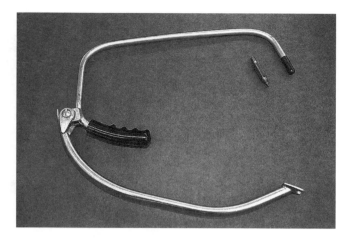

*This bulls-eye pick is a very accurate way to raise low spots, and is relatively easy to get into tight spots. Ron sells a soft, non-metallic tip that's handy for aluminum and lighter sheet steel.*

*Ron places the "female" part of the pick over the low spot and then brings the handle up fairly gently to rap the panel from the bottom and raise the low spot.*

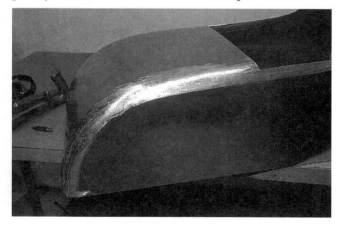

*Though you can always go farther, the welded seam is essentially finished.*

*To begin the process of making a hammerform, Ron marks out an outline on the MDF with a sanding disc of the right diameter.*

*With the outline marked on the MDF, Ron cuts out the shape with the band saw.*

work I needed to keep busy. Basically, he put me into business in a totally painless way.

For about the first ten years I did almost nothing but build dragster bodies. Then after that I got interested in the world of street rods. I did a job for a man named Tom Prufer building a track roadster from the ground up that got wonderful publicity. It's still a very well known and popular car. That's mostly where I've done my work over the years - in the street rod arena.

*So you've always been self-employed?*

Yes. I did take a break to go to school to study art in the middle of all that. After I graduated I continued working at the school half-time. I was the supervisor for the shop in the art department. But that's the only other job I've ever had.

*Of all the stuff that you learned, maybe primarily from Arnie, what would you consider the most valuable lessons?*

Hang in there. Stay with it. If it seems difficult, realize that other people have had to work through the rough spots to develop their skills to the point where they have a success rather than a failure.

*You use hammerforming for a lot of your metal shaping. Can you talk about the advantages and disadvantages of that particular way of shaping metal?*

I didn't learn about

The edges are sanded lightly to eliminate any roughness before the piece is taken over to the router.

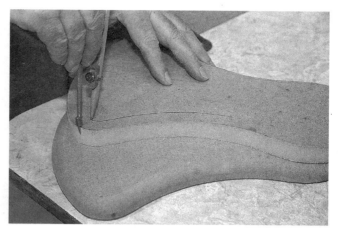

The clamping block must be cut smaller than the inner radius of the hammerform.

A clean, round edge is created with the router, all the way around the edge of the hammerform.

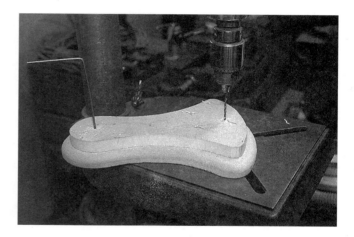

With the clamping block in the correct position, the drill press is used to drill holes for the alignment pins.

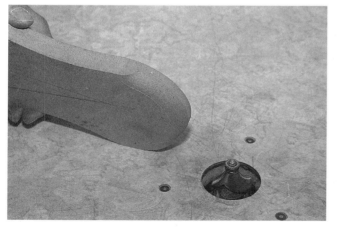

This close up shows the router mounted on its own table and the nice radiused edge it leaves in the MDF.

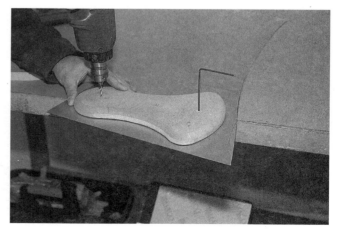

Next, the clamping block is placed above the raw aluminum so matching holes can be drilled in the sheet metal.

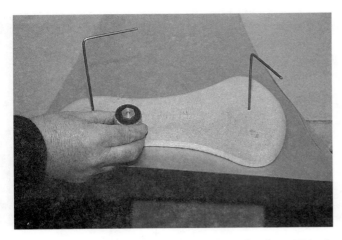

*This is the small tool that Ron uses to mark a line 5/8inch outside the edge of the hammerform.*

*Ron uses the band saw to cut out the aluminum to the proper size.*

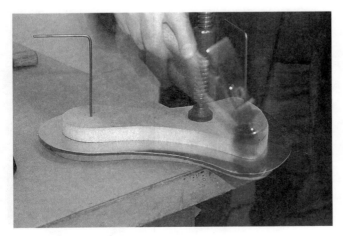

*After making a sandwich with the aluminum and two pieces of MDF, Ron starts shaping the metal with a hammer.*

hammerforming until about 12 years ago. So since I've been working about 35 years, most of the work I had done was without the benefit of hammerforms. I learned about the process from Ron Fournier's books on metal working. Once I tried it, I just saw that it was the perfect solution for so many situations that metal workers encounter: Once the tooling is made you can make parts very easily. In many cases, it makes parts that look sort of store-bought or die stamped. Often you can eliminate all tooling marks. If the majority of the part is flat with simply some shape on the edge, it's an ideal way to work the material. The only disadvantage is it takes a little time to make the hammerform. But in most cases, it's a very fast process.

*So the time spent making the hammerform is time well spent and time that in the long run you'd probably spend on the project anyway?*

In many cases. I very often will make a hammerform for one article. Of course, if you're making 10 or 50 or 100, it makes perfect sense. But even for a one-off, it sometimes makes sense.

*Back to the hammerform a little bit. You said one of the advantages is that it's a better way to shrink?*

Yeah. It's not too hard to bend metal with a hammer and dolly, and it's relatively easy to stretch metal with a hammer and dolly, but to make metal shrink you can only do a very, very limited amount of shrinking using just a hammer and dolly. If you add heat, you can do a lot of shrinking with heat, a hammer, and a dolly, but it's difficult to control it accurately. The beauty of the hammerform is that usually hammerforms are made of a material that's easy to shape like wood or maybe a soft metal like aluminum. Once you have the proper shape introduced to the hammerform, it's dead simple just to move the metal down until it touches the hammerform continuously. Very, very easy process. That's the real beauty of it.

*You do a bunch of workshops. What do you try to convey to the students? What's the most important thing that you want them to take from that workshop?*

I think what I really focus on is how much good work you can do with the simplest of tools. The point I try to make is there are wonderful tools that are expensive like power hammers and wheeling machines, and they're well-suited to their purpose. But if you can't afford those machines or are not yet at the point in your career where you want to buy them, you can do it all with hand tools. All the Ferraris and Maserattis from the early 1960s were built using just hand tools. It's just a matter of gaining enough skill with them to make whatever part you want.

*So what's the minimum tools that a person needs to at least begin doing some work at home?*

I would say a set of good hammers and dollies, a mallet, a sandbag, something to weld with - probably an oxyacetylene welder to start, and something to cut the metal with. That's really about all you need.

*Do people at home need little shrinkers? Shrinker/stretchers?*

It's probably going to be the best $150 you ever spent for a sheet metal tool. The bigger ones are nice, but even the inexpensive ones with the one inch deep throat can do a tremendous amount of work. The vast majority of the shrinking you need to do can be done just at the edge. A lot of times if you just shrink the edge it will influence the metal as much as two inches away from the edge. It'll do some shrinking even that deep into the panel.

*Do you have a strong preference for steel or aluminum or does it depend on the project?*

In terms of shaping metal, I much prefer working with aluminum. I call it the "friendly metal." Ron Fournier calls it a confidence builder, because it simply can be put into whatever shape you want with much less force and much less effort than with steel. But for certain situations, steel is a better choice. One example, in fact, is motorcycle fenders, especially rigid frames in particular or an engine that vibrates a lot, like most of the V-twins do. Aluminum fenders have a reputation for failing from cracking with vibration, so that's one situation where steel might be superior. Of course, I'm not always making things from new metal. Very often people will bring a car to me and want something modified on it, and most cars are made from steel so you're pretty much forced to work with steel. But for building things from scratch, alu-

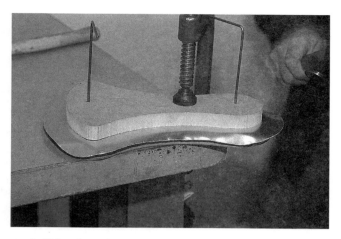

*In half-hard condition, the corners are very resistant to any shaping.*

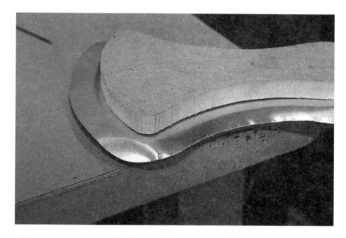

*Here you can see the limited amount of shaping Ron was able to do without annealing the metal.*

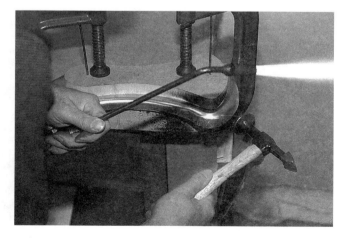

*After annealing the metal is much easier to shape, though the sharpest part of the corners require more heat to further soften the aluminum and allow Ron to finish the piece.*

83

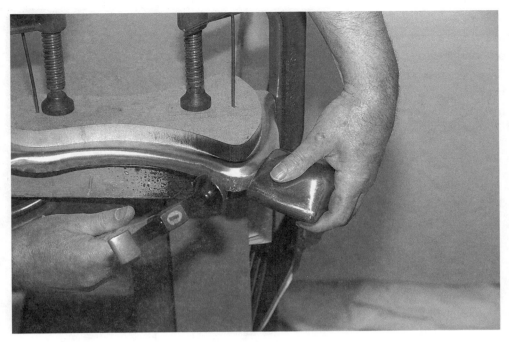

*By using a dolly across the corner from the area Ron is hammering, the force of the hammer blows are concentrated under the hammer head.*

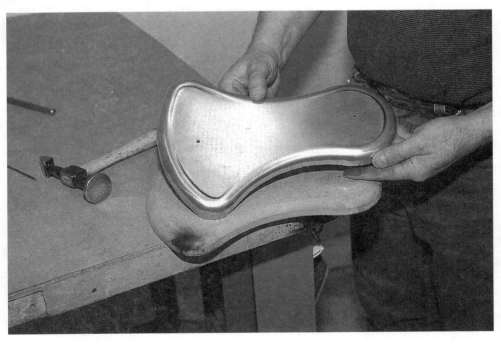

*The finished piece, with just a little soot left on the surface from the annealing process.*

minum is nearly always my first choice.

*Are welding skills essential to any kind of serious metal fabrication?*

Well, it depends. When you look at the construction of aircraft, there is very little welding involved with those. Mostly they use high strength alloys and they design the joints so they are riveted together. Now they are often bonded together, like on the big 747s. So that's one class of metal working that doesn't necessarily require welding skills. But for most practical automotive or motorcycle projects, you need to weld the parts sooner or later. Said another way, it's rare that a part can be made from a single piece of metal. Sometimes it happens, but more often, you'll have to join several pieces, and welding is a way to make joints that can become absolutely invisible if you want to metal finish them.

*What do you prefer - gas or heli-arc?*

I TIG weld almost everything these days and have for about the last 15 years. But for people at home they can get by with an oxyacetylene outfit. I would recommend an oxy-acetylene even over a MIG welder. MIG welding is used a lot. It's a good process; it's a fast process; it makes a sound weld; the welders themselves are not particularly expensive compared with TIG welders, but the disadvantage of a MIG weld is once it's in place, you almost can't do anything with it.

Welding always shrinks and on a sheet metal panel the shrinkage usually makes the weld area sink in relation to the metal around it. With the TIG welder, or an oxyacetylene weld, you can compress the metal of the weld, hammering it against a dolly, and if you hammer it just the right amount, it will come right back where it came from. The MIG weld is so strong, so hard, and so brittle, that if you hammer it that much it probably will fail before it comes back up to where it came from. So the only thing wrong with MIG welding is that if you are going to use a MIG welder, you'll probably have to use some sort of filler on top of the weld. I'm not an enemy of filler. It really has its place, and as long as you don't abuse filler, it's a good material. I just have a preference for working things out in the metal. It's kind of a craftsman's issue rather than a styling issue.

*I asked once before, but what's the most important lesson that a beginning fabricator needs to learn? Patience?*

I think persistence. Anyone who has worked with metal for a while learns that it doesn't come easily. Every now and then there's a superstar who picks it up overnight, but that's extremely rare. Most people are very frustrated

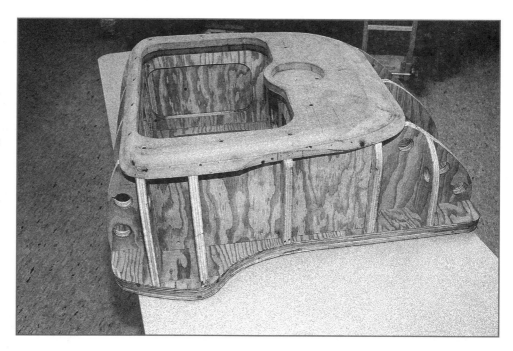

*This is the combination hammerform and buck that Ron is using to form the cowling for an airplane.*

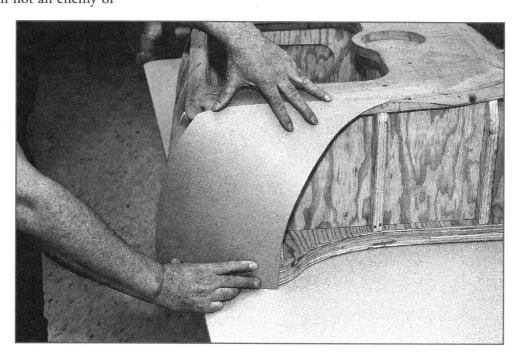

*A light-board template is cut to size as the first step in this process.*

After cutting out the metal to match the template, Ron starts by shaping the metal by hand.

Here you can see better the shape of the lower wheel. Ron is making another series of passes through the wheel with light pressure between the wheels to finish or planish the metal.

A test fit of the panel to see where it needs the most shape.

The wheel puts a compound curve on the sheet of aluminum.

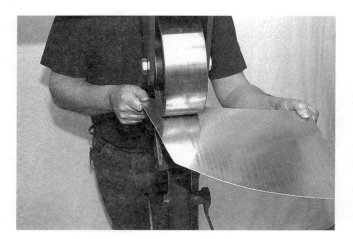

To crown the metal Ron runs it through the English wheel, with a mildly crowned lower (or anvil) wheel in place. If you look closely you can see the "tracks" left by the wheel.

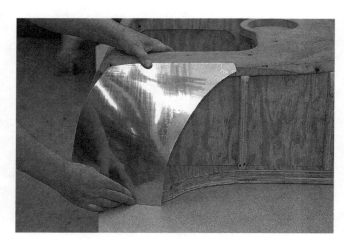

No longer just a bent piece of metal, the piece is now mildly domed. Note the bright finish the metal picked up from the polished upper wheel.

learning the process of working metal with hand tools. You have to find your way with it. There are going to be lots of failures and lots of times where you're feeling stuck. Lots of times when you want the metal to behave a certain way and it just doesn't. It has its own mind about what it's going to do. But in time, if you stick with it, you start learning the tricks. You start learning the subtle things that you do with the hammer and dolly to allow the metal to form in a way that you want it to rather than what it wants to. It takes a lot of persistence.

*As you become more familiar with working metal are you able to predict how far away the metal is affected.*

I think you do get better at predicting how it's going to react to shrinking or stretching. There's a lot of factors involved - the material thickness, whether it's been annealed or not, how hard it was from the mill, what you're using to shrink it with. You know the foot-powered shrinkers just have more force than the hand-powered shrinkers, and there are power shrinkers that are even stronger than that. The shape of the panel is probably the greatest determinant of what the results will be. In other words, if a panel is shaped like half a basketball, it's going to behave differently from a flat sheet when you shrink the edge.

*Anything else you want to add or convey?*

I guess the only thing I would add is that it seems like there's this big mystique built up around metal working. I mean I think most people probably think that if they wanted to learn the skills used by a carpenter, as long as they have decent hand and eye coordination, that's something they could learn. Whereas with metal work, many people think that's just out of the question, they say, 'I could never learn that.' And from my point of view, the skills required for carpentry are pretty much the same skills required to be a good metal worker. You need to have patience. You need to learn the problem-solving steps to accomplish a big task by breaking it into a bunch of small tasks, and you need hand and eye coordination and development of your skills. That's it.

Now, with a much more crowned anvil wheel in place, Ron uses the English wheel to put a tight radius on the edge of the metal.

To eliminate ripples in areas where there is too much metal, Ron does some limited shrinking.

The finished piece, ready to be mated up and welded to the rest of the cowling.

# Chapter Six

# No Power Tools

## Bob Munroe, Working for the King

Arlen Ness is often called the King of Custom Motorcycles. The bikes themselves are made up of some lovely flowing shapes all fabricated from steel and aluminum. If you ask Arlen specific questions about his bikes, like who made the wonderful "bas-

ket of snakes" exhaust for Two Bad over 20 years ago, or who crafted the beautiful fenders on the more recent Arrow bike, the answer is always the same: "The Mun," a.k.a. Bob Munroe.

Thus it only seems appropriate that Bob Munroe

*Part way through the process, Bob's aluminum fender, placed carefully over the simple buck he used to* *ensure the fender will fit the bike exactly like it's supposed to.*

would fabricate a motorcycle part for our demonstration sequence. The project seen here is the creation of a rear motorcycle fender, formed with help from an existing buck. Like many of these projects Bob Munroe begins not with a piece of steel or aluminum, but with a piece of paper. "The paper will tell me where I need to start," explains Bob.

Though he does use heavier chip-board for some applications, for this situation Bob makes the pattern from some very light paper.

Bob cuts the paper to size, just a little bigger than he thinks the piece of metal should be, and then cuts a curve into the paper along the two longest sides, explaining as he does, "I've found that if I take the straight edge off the paper it helps it to form to the shape, the paper will lay down better than it would if it had a straight edge."

Using the paper as a template, Bob marks a piece of aluminum to be cut. The aluminum used here is 3003, H14, .063inches thick, though .050inch could be used for this fender. Though we tend to think of aluminum as too fragile or prone to cracking to make a good motorcycle fender, Bob reports he's never had a problem. "People who have trouble with cracking are mounting them wrong," says Bob. "Or using the wrong material or not finishing the edge off with a doubler or an edge-wire." The piece of aluminum is cut in the band saw. Bob cuts it slightly bigger than it needs to be, and then takes the torch and anneals the aluminum.

About building the form, Bob explains, "I cut the back bone out right over the tire, allowing for three inches of clearance. Then I start adding my shapes on the sides. What's hard is deciding how to make the part taper, and how much, and then how to make each station. The better the buck, with more stations, the better off you are. Sometimes though, if I'm in a hurry to get the buck done and start shaping I don't add as many stations as I might."

Bob starts by holding the aluminum over the buck, just a rough positioning. The hammer Bob picks up is chosen for its shape, actually a rather mild crown on the wooden head. The first round of work is done with the wooden hammer, pounding on the aluminum which is positioned over a large leather bag filled with sand.

It takes a fair amount of hammering, and frequent checking on the buck, to get the flat sheet of alu-

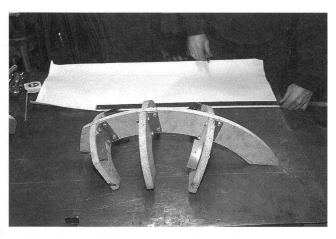

*Bob's buck isn't elaborate, just good enough to show the shape and give him something to fit the emerging fender up against.*

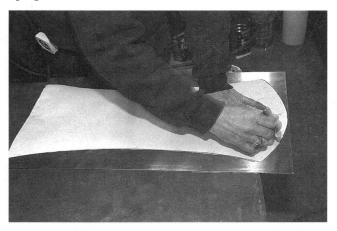

*After he has a paper template that roughly fits the buck, Bob uses that to mark out the sheet metal.*

*Because the entire piece will be shaped, Bob anneals the entire surface of the aluminum sheet.*

The work starts with nothing more elaborate than a large wooden hammer and a leather bag of sand.

Bob stacks up the two bags, with the shot filled bag positioned on top, and positions the fender so he's rolling in the edges more.

Bob works the hammer along the center of the fender and gradually it begins to take on a shape.

Though the methods seem too simple, in less than an hour Bob has the sheet of aluminum looking like the beginnings of a fender.

Checked against the buck, the fender has a long way to go.

After the test fit it's obvious the fender needs more stretching and more shape, provided here with the wooden mallet.

minum to look like a fender. And there are times, mid-way through the project, when it seems the piece has such a bad case of "walnuts" that it will never turn into anything useful. But Bob persists, undeterred by the roughness of the metal during certain parts of the operation. Eventually a fender begins to emerge from the sheet of aluminum.

When he's got the basic shape roughed out, Bob makes the comment that, "a guy could wheel it out the rest of the way, but I'm going to just keep on 'bagging.'" At this poin, Bob goes back to the little bag filled with lead, which is his favorite, instead of the other which is filled with sand.

Along the edges Bob uses a rawhide hammer, working against a wood base, to shrink the edges, explaining as he does, "If you did this with steel it would stretch the metal." Then it's back to the big wooden hammer, though the blows are made with a certain finesse. "We've got the rough shape now," explains Bob. "So I'm not hitting it as hard, I'm starting to take the lumps out."

So far all this has been done with nothing more than a hammer and a bag of shot.

Now Bob uses a wooden slapper and a dolly to roll the edges more and have them pull in tight against the buck. Serious bulges develop along the sides of the fender, an indication that there is too much material along the sides.

The buck is used as a checking device and Bob often places the metal on the buck, checks his progress, and then goes back to hammering or even shaping with his hands. Now Bob begins to use the wheel to take out some of the lumps and bumps, with pretty light pressure on the rollers. "The problem," explains Bob, "is that the rolling will open up the fender more." After a test fit Bob goes back to the wheel with a little more pressure. The anvil wheel Bob is using is one with a radius close to the shape of the fender.

Bob shrinks the fender on the small shrinker until it fits good front to back, but it is still too loose, not tight, on the sides. Bob wheels it more and more across the fender in the short direction.

Though the piece is starting to look like a fender, the edges still won't come around, so Bob goes back to the hammer and the bag of shot. The next step is to switch to the wooden slapper and the dolly, to roll the edges in more.

*Progress comes steadily. Bulges along the sides indicate areas where there's too much metal.*

*The wooden slapper is used to roll the edges of the fender in more, working in tandem with a dolly held on the inside of the fender.*

*Not a thing of beauty, but look back just a few pictures to see how far we've come.*

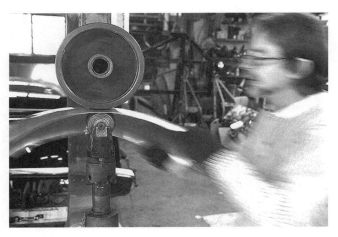

*At this point Bob slides the fender between the rollers of his English wheel. The lower wheel has quite a bit of crown, as does the fender.*

*It's simply magic. That lump of walnuts is not only smooth, but looking like a fender.*

*Bob puts the fender back into the wheel, the short way, to give it more shape and smooth out more of the bumps.*

Metal shaping often seems like "three steps forward and two back." The last step Bob performed opened the fender up the long way, so now it must be shrunk on the sides so that it comes into a tighter radius over the wheel. In describing this point in the progress Bob says, "it's a back and forth deal." Now it fits pretty good in both directions, but of course it's lumpy again, so Bob goes back to the wheel to smooth it out.

Bob takes a few lumps out with the mallet over the bag of lead, then goes to the wheel. More trial fit, more wheel work. Now Bob is essentially happy with the fender and feels it's time to make the fender sides.

As always, Bob starts by making another pattern from paper that he cuts slightly oversize. Bob holds it up, marks the edge and trims it to size. Now he cuts two pieces of metal on the band saw and files the edges. After checking the basic fit of the panels, Bob gets out the torch and prepares to anneal the panels explaining, "I'm going to anneal these, you maybe wouldn't have to, they don't have a lot of shape, but annealing the metal will make it shape faster and easier."

In order to ensure that the fender won't move on the buck as he forms and attaches the side panels, Bob drills two small holes on each side of the fender and installs two Clecos, or temporary rivets, that attach through to brackets already in place on the buck.

The shaping of the side panel starts with a slap hammer working over the bag of sand, When it becomes obvious that there's too much metal bunching up at the edge Bob goes to the shrinker.

Then he works it with the slapper made of wood with a leather cover. Next, Bob moves to the wheel and then checks the fit. The metal has a ways to go, so Bob hits it with the steel slap hammer along the edge.

At this point the side panel is close to being right. Bob slides it up under the fender, marks the edge with a felt-tip marker, and then trims the excess metal with the tin snips. Not completely satisfied, Bob goes through three or four more trim-shrink-slap sequences until the side panel fits up against the buck and the fender really nice.

Before doing any welding Bob cleans off the marks on the edge of the side panel so nothing can contaminate the weld, and files the edges. "I used to weld with gas," says Bob. "even for aluminum, but the bikes I work on now usually have the wheels and the engine installed, and it's all billet aluminum and the flux from gas welding is really messy. So I've gone to heli-arc welding partly because it's so much neater."

The first welds are just small tack welds. "I use 1100 pure aluminum rods," explains Bob. "It used to be when I would file the weld, the weld was harder than the aluminum around it and I'd file and file and the weld never got any smaller. Finally I switched to the 1100 rod and that makes it easier to file the welds."

Now Bob works the welds with the slap hammer over a fixture, then raises low areas by hammering against the seam from the inside with a leather mallet while holding the fender against a leather bag of sand. After massaging the seam Bob adds more welds.

Next, he raises a low spot by pounding on the inside. Then he takes a high speed grinder and knocks off the lumps on the inside of the fender explaining, "the inside of the seam needs to be smooth or you can't rest the dolly against the whole surface as you hammer on it from the other side." Once the inside of the fender is smooth we can start to planish that area with a hammer and dolly. Part of the seam is low, so Bob raises that area with a crowned hammer from the inside.

Then he tries to smooth out the area with the slap hammer while holding a dolly against the seam from the inside. Bob hammers the areas that are high, then runs his hand over it, hammers more, then runs his hand over it again.

(Note: Bob is using a dolly underneath and the slap hammer for this part of the operation - note the photo of the dolly and the hammer)

Now Bob knocks the top off the welds on the outside, then the skirted area is run through the wheel to further smooth out that area.

It's somewhat easier to wheel the fender now because the skirt helps the fender to hold it's shape. Once the shape is correct Bob goes ahead and does the final welding of the seam.

Because this is aluminum and the tack welds are fairly close together Bob feels he can weld it continuously, "it won't 'lump up' or warp like steel will. Now I will run the torch through the inside of the bead,

*To tighten up the radius of the whole fender Bob shrinks the edges on both sides.*

*Though the fender looks good it isn't tight enough to the buck along the sides, so the next step is more work on the wheel.*

*Bob runs it back and forth the short way, to raise the center, and thus tighten up the sides.*

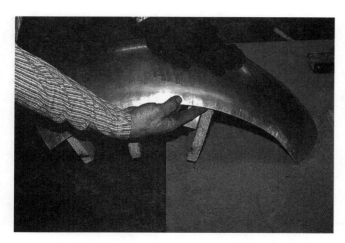

*A test fit shows that the sides still haven't come down tight enough against the buck.*

*So it's back on the wheel the short way to give the fender more shape.*

*Frustrated with the progress, Bob goes back to the simplest of tools, the wooden mallet and the bag of shot.*

called a 'burn down,' to eliminate the ridge of what was molten aluminum on the inside of the weld. This is done with no rod." The "after" photo of the inside shows how the former ridge has been turned into a seamless smooth flow of aluminum.

Now Bob sands the outside of the bead explaining, "I used to use a Vixen file, but now I use a small grinder with a 36 grit pad. If you use a lot of WD 40 on the pad it won't load up with aluminum filings, and the process is much faster than the file."

From here you could take the finishing as far as you want, "I might want to do the rest of the finish work with a hammer and dolly." For our purposes the hand work and hammering have resulted in the creation of a fender.

### BOB MUNROE INTERVIEW

*Bob, can we talk about your history? How you got started in the fabrication business.*

Well, like most teens I knew hot rod cars was where I wanted to be. I started buying car magazines when I was pretty young. I'd open those pages and I'd see them chopping a top or Frenching headlights, and that's what I wanted to do. So I went where people were doing that stuff. Jim Davis lived near me (the late Jim Davis, chassis builder from Walnut Creek, California) and he had those hot rod cars, and I just started hanging out there.

In about 1964 I started working at a shop where they built fire trucks. I learned a lot of sheet metal fabrication at the fire truck facility. No shaping as we know it, but like that tool box, I built that while I was there. After a lay-off I went to work in a body shop. Then Art Himsl expanded his paint business and needed somebody to do some light customizing. That was right up my alley. Later I went to work for Pete Ogden, he had plenty of work in a fabrication shop working on race cars and midgets.

Pete taught me a lot. He taught me the heli-arc, and then the aluminum work. Eventually I landed at Jim Davis' shop helping him build dragsters. I learned a lot working for Davis, that was good.

*So that was your inspiration to begin doing sheet metal fabrication?*

When we'd finish with a chassis the car would go to a shop where they built the bodies. Most of those went to Jack Hagemann. Back then the way it went there was on the roof of Jim's station wagon. A chassis would fit on the roof, overhanging the front. Even when the front engine cars got real long a bare chas-

To force the sides to roll in more Bob uses the wooden slapper on the outside working against the dolly held on the inside of the fender.

Another in the endless series of test fits.

A test fit shows that while the fender fits better on the sides, it has opened up the long way.

To take out the lumps from the hammering Bob puts the fender back into the wheel and works it the long way.

Shrinking the sides near the front and back of the fender will help to tighten it up the long way.

Satisfied with the shape of the basic fender, it's time to make a paper template for the sides of the fender.

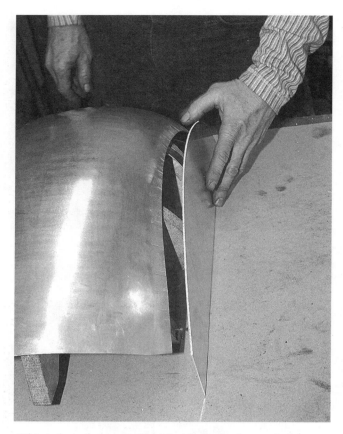

*This is how far away the sides of the fender are before Bob starts to shape the side panels.*

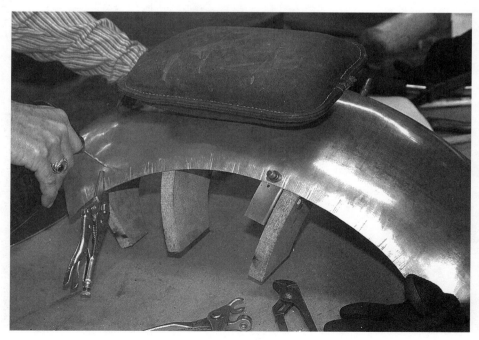

*Cleco, spring-loaded rivets, are used to hold the fender to the buck and keep it in place as the sides are fabricated and fit.*

sis could be hauled on the roof. That's how they got to Hag's. That was before covered trailers. That's when racing was cool. A flat open trailer with that car on it. That was just the best.

I'd go along to deliver the chassis in order to see the work they were doing in that shop, and that just did it for me. Once in a while we took a car to Arnie Roberts. Same thing. Boy, I didn't want to miss out on that. I wanted to see what these guys are doing,

From there, I came here to my own shop. Arlen Ness came along about that time. We did the frames first and then Arlen needed oil tanks and gas tanks and knick knacks. That was it. Pretty soon I'm evolving into better stuff. These aluminum bodied bikes, and then lately the Harley car. This stuff has just really been good for me. I've been learning and getting paid while I learn.

*Do you want to talk a little bit about steel versus aluminum and how you decide which one to use for a project? The pros and cons of steel and aluminum.*

Normally, if somebody comes in here and wants a custom gas tank made for their bike, the reason they're coming here for it is because they want an aluminum tank. The aluminum tanks work fine on anything with a rubber mounted motor, like a Harley FXR or Dyna. And actually it's easier to shape than steel, so for making something streamlined it just works out better.

But as you can see on my own bikes, I chose steel for the tank on the antique bike. Because I finally, after all these years of beating my brains out doing this stuff, I finally learned to use that A-K steel (aluminum-killed), which is soft enough to shape, almost as easily as aluminum. All these years I made all those tanks out of 16 gauge, that's almost plate. So anyway... just in the last year I found out where to get this A-K steel and it's fine for that stuff.

Me being a fabricator, on my own bike I want a nice aluminum oil tank. The ones I did on the other two antique bikes were steel, and the ones I do on any-

96

Bob annealed this entire sheet of aluminum to make it easier to shape. Here he starts on the edge with the slapper.

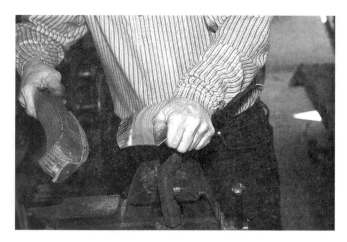

To further encourage the edge to roll in Bob uses the wooden slapper.

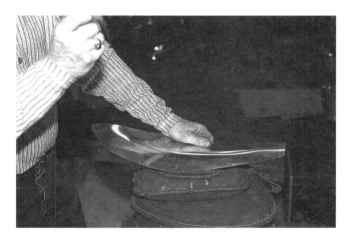

By using the slapper along the radius of the new side panel Bob is able to roll the entire thing in.

Before finishing with the side panel, Bob puts it in the wheel to eliminate any roughness left from the earlier work, and to crown it further.

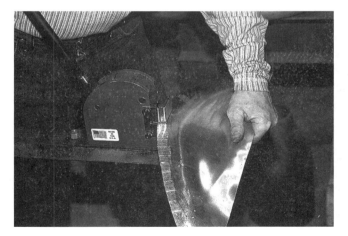

But of course there's too much metal, necessitating a round of shrinking.

And then there's just a little more adjusting to do....

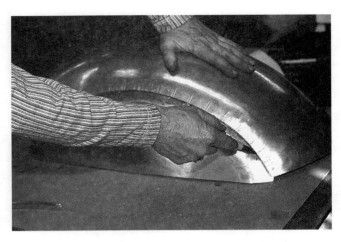

....before the piece is deemed good enough and Bob can mark the edge where the two pieces meet.

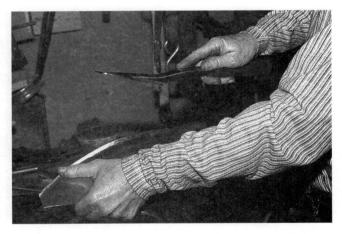

To get a bit more shape at the edge of the side panel Bob works it with a slap hammer.

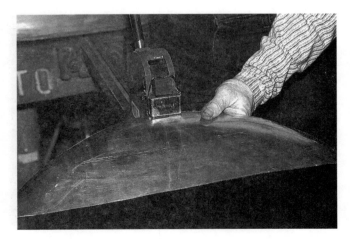

And then shrinks the upper edge to add crown to the top of the side panel.

thing that comes in here for a customer is steel. So steel for oil tanks is the norm really. And fenders are almost always aluminum.

*So the metal depends on the project?*

Yeah. If a guy comes in with a hot rod and wants a hood on a Deuce Roadster, that's aluminum. Nobody's going to make it out of steel. If somebody wants to get a hood made for their car, they want the hood made out of aluminum.

*You don't have any trouble with aluminum cracking? Even on motorcycles?*

No. Never had a problem there. I'm trying to think. There have been gas tank leaks due to vibration from rigid-mounted motors rather than rubber mounted motors, and guys not mounting the tank properly. They don't shim it and get everything bolted up right. It has to mount so it's well supported and there's no stress on the tank.

*You don't use a lot of tools. Some guys use power hammers and English wheels and you tend to work with a hammer and a bag of shot.*

I have room problems. If I had more room and something was available, I would move up in tools. But knowing it can be done by hand, I'm in no hurry. There are a lot of guys that can make it by hand in the same amount of time as a guy who uses that big equipment. So just knowing it can be done that way is fine with me. I'll continue to work with hand tools.

*Can you talk a little bit about the process you go through on the more elaborate fabrication projects? Do you get a rendering, and then you make a buck, and then you start to fabricate?*

Originally Arlen and I would just talk it over. We'd say, 'let's just put a fender on this or do a gas tank and stretch it out.' We'd just talk it through. We had no drawings. Arlen would do a simple sketch to convey to me what he hand in mind. And that worked. But then Carl Brouhad came along, Carl's drawings are just the best. He takes a photograph of the frame and then he blows that photograph up and does the drawing of the body panels on that chassis photo so it's all to scale.

Once I get a drawing from him, I can almost measure from his drawing. Carl has really improved our methods, due to the quality of the renderings.

*But the renderings are not full size?*

No. They're not full size and they're always just a side view. So when he does give us one of these I have no idea what that fender's supposed to look like in three dimensions. I didn't know if that fender has a

A test fit shows a good match between the side panel and the fender.

Bob uses a die-grinder to eliminate the ridge on the inside of each tack weld. This way the inside surface is smooth enough to correctly support a dolly.

Which means it's time for the first tack welds, done with 1100 rod.

Though the fit is good, there are low spots along the tack-welded seam.

After tack welding the fender together Bob knocks down the worst of the high spots.

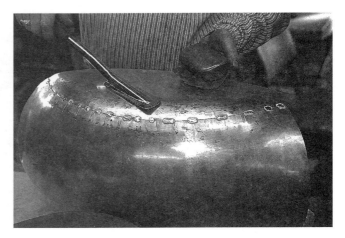

With a hammer and dolly Bob smoothes out the seam before he does the final welding.

*A coarse file is used to knock off the worst of the high spots and the tops of the tack welds.*

*With the tops off the tack welds Bob can run the fender through the English wheel. Because of the sides the fender isn't likely to change shape at this point.*

peak in it. I just opted for the peak. Who knows. You got a side view. I didn't know if it was flat or round, because he doesn't give you what I call a perspective. No top view of a gas tank or fender. So I just take that on my own, which works with Arlen just fine.

*So you end up with a lot of artistic freedom?*

Absolutely. I very seldom have to change anything. If I have my doubts about something I'll call. We touch base just about every night unless he's out of town.

*How did you learn to build a buck?*

I just saw them as pictures in books. There's numerous books with pictures of a complete sports car bodies made out of plywood with all these little stations every four or five inches. You don't hammer on a buck. You just fit your material to it. Jack Hagemann has some out there for Scarabs that are just a piece of work. But the ones you see here, I just spend enough time to get going. If I thought I'd like a nice set of aluminum fenders on my car there, because you can't buy those fenders, I'd probably spend as much time on the buck as on the fender. But then you always have it and you're not going to wear it out if you build it right, because you don't hammer on it. You just fit to it. A lot of times a guy won't even Cleco the part to the buck like you saw me doing. You just fit, overlap, draw a line, sticker it, trim it, lay it on there, and tack it.

That gas tank on that big red Arrow bike - I did that without a buck. I just started with the top of the tank, rolled it down to the neck, notched it out to fit over the top bar and the back of it. I spaced it up off the frame with a chunk of clay and that held it taut. I had it shaped the way I liked. I had a peak in it. Then I started hitting the sides right on the bike. I built that from aluminum with no buck.

*Do you make paper templates a lot?*

I use paper all the time rather than chip board. It lays down good. This particular paper I'm using has a different texture, it'll lay down good. You can slit it with a razor to overlap it. That's where you would have to shrink your material. Areas where the paper is bunched up, you know that's where you have to get rid of metal.

*So the buck comes first and then the paper goes over the buck?*

Yeah. Sometimes I won't even paper. Maybe that's because I've done enough of it where I feel confident now. Patterns are good though.

*Is an artistic eye necessary?*

Yeah. You have to have it. If you don't have it going in, I don't think you'd ever pick it up. As a kid in school I would doodle and draw cars on my book covers, dragsters, hot rods and roadsters. I was always into drawing. But creativity too, I could always make stuff. Most guys that do this stuff are creative, and have a sense of how things should look.

*You need a sense of form?*

Exactly. An idea of what would work with the components that are already there. I don't know if that comes with time. Some people I don't think ever pick that up.

*Given all your time in the business, if you were going to pass along one bit of information to somebody learning the trade what would it be?*

You've got to get hands-on. You've got to do it. Working for somebody good would be the best. I never worked for anybody that really knew this stuff as well as I would have liked. Like Ron Covell or Steve Davis. That's where you would pick it up.

If you were young and just going in to learn a trade, four or five years with someone like that and you'd be on your own. I just keep telling people, 'I'm still working through it.' Patience is a lot of it. You can't get in too big of a hurry. I've learned to slow down a lot. I've been overworking the metal, I almost did that today. Keep working and working and working. I get to spending so much time on several of these, it was better an hour ago. There are some good classes now from Ron Covell, Fay Butler, and Fournier.

Note the nice smooth transition from fender to fender-side. Now it's time for the final welding.

After the seam is welded Bob does most of the finishing with a small grinder equipped with a 36 grit pad. Plenty of WD 40 keeps things cool and prevents the aluminum from loading up the sanding disc.

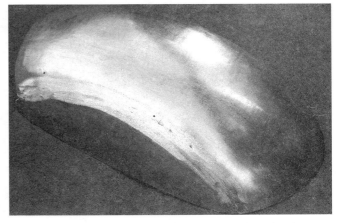

The finished piece. Hard to believe that only a few hours earlier this fender didn't exist.

## Chapter Seven

# With Just a Hammer & a Wheel

# Bo's Hand-Built Fender

Though Bo Olson from Stillwater, Minnesota is a "fabricator" he's more than that, even as measured against other fabricators. Part body man and part blacksmith Bo Olson works on everything from Bentlys to Model T Fords.

When pressed he can even be persuaded to make a fender for a certain book publisher named Remus.

The project Bo chose is the fabrication of the front half of a fender from scratch. To move

*In the foreground, the front half of the new fender crafted by hand. Behind it, the fender that was used as a template, in place of a formal buck.*

things along fairly quickly Bo decided to made the fender from aluminum sheet instead of steel.

As Bo explains, "We're going to do this complete section in one piece. But some people would do it in two pieces, some might even do it in three, one central dome and the two sides. The bigger the piece the harder it is to form." For Bo, the first step is to cut the piece out on the saw.

Before beginning on the big piece of aluminum sheet, however, Bo cuts a small piece of the same material and "test drives it" in both the shrinker and the wheel to see exactly how this metal is going to work.

During the planning part of the operation, Bo realizes that the problem with making this piece of a fender is the fact that as he stretches the center, or main part, of the fender the edges are going to curl and crinkle. The wrinkles indicate an excess of metal which means Bo will have to stretch the metal through the center and shrink the sides.

To get things moving along fairly quickly Bo's first step is with the plastic hammer, working the metal over the leather covered bag of sand. "You can't be afraid to make it move," explains Bo, "working it with the plastic hammer will give it direction right away."

The next step is to run the sheet of aluminum through the English wheel the long way, over and over, and then turn it 90 degrees. The wheel gives the piece a nice concave shape, like a trough, and smoothes out the lumps from the first round of hammering.

To further stretch the metal, and begin forming the "dome" at the top of the fender, Bo goes back to working the piece with the plastic hammer and the bag of sand, stopping occasionally to test the fit of the piece over the existing fender we're using as a buck. Then it's more hammer work until Bo decides it's time to do some shrinking along the two long sides or edges.

Next, the planishing hammer is used to smooth out some of the lumps left from the work

*Behind the raw piece of aluminum sheet is the existing fender Bo will duplicate.*

*Bo starts on the new fender with the plastic hammer, the sand bag is placed underneath. In hindsight he feels the hammer could have been used more aggressively early on.*

*After running it through the wheel the long way Bo turns the metal 90 degrees and runs it through again. Note how much shape the metal already has.*

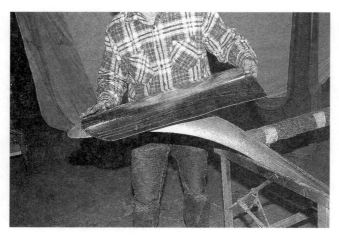

It's never too early for a test fit. Though the metal has taken on some crown, there's no sign yet of the curve the metal must assume in order to mimic the shape of the fender.

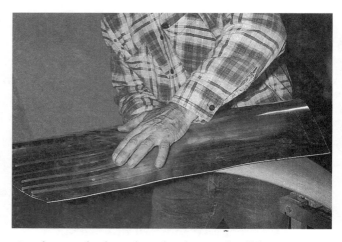

Another test fit shows how far the metal still has to go.

The straight edge shows the degree to which the metal was shaped so far.

To help form the curve over the top of the tire Bo begins shrinking the sides.

To form a dome Bo begins to further stretch the metal with the plastic hammer working over a bag of sand.

The planishing hammer is used to raise up a smaller area and to smooth out the lumps left from the earlier hammer work.

done with the plastic hammer, and also lift the area in the center of the fender.

Now Bo moves the fender to the shrinker, working mostly at the nose. "This puts stress on the panel," explains Bo, "at the edges, so it will force the metal to take the shape I'm after."

The piece is beginning to look like a fender, it's starting to fit our "buck" though there's a kink in the sides. Bo puts it back on the wheel and runs it through the long way and then moves back to the leather bag.

Time now for more beating with the plastic hammer to raise the domed area at the front of the fender, the part of the fender with the most crown, followed by another test fit, and more hammering.

Bo spends considerable time at this point trying to determine where the metal needs to move, and what is the best way to make it do exactly that. After a few more hammer blows Bo does another test fit. Now he shrinks the edges on the Erco shrinker. "The shrinking helps get rid of the wrinkles on the side," says Bo, "and those wrinkles are fighting me."

The shrinking is followed by more hammering with the plastic mallet and another test fit.

More hammering now, still primarily in the central part of the new fender tip. "It takes a lot of stretching to hump that fender up like that," says Bo, "more than a guy realizes." So it's back on the wheel, running it the long way, to take out the walnuts and to stretch it further. At this point Bo comments that, "you can actually see the low areas raise up as you run the piece through the wheel." Now another test fit and then a break.

This second little analysis session indicates the need for more shape at the nose so Bo stretches the metal further with the hammer working at the front of the fender. The hammer work is followed by more wheeling, the short way this time.

Then it's more hammer work at the nose again, which leaves a low spot behind the area that Bo just worked. "You can see where we've raised the metal just in from the edge," explains Bo. "So now there's a low spot behind it."

*Now Bo shrinks at the front of the fender to put stress on that part of the fender and help to force up the dome.*

*The test fit shows a piece of sheet metal that's starting to look like a fender, with a proper nose and some of the shape Bo is after.*

*More stretching and smoothing on the wheel, followed by another test fit.*

The plastic hammer is brought into play again, primarily in the area that will form the dome over the top of the tire.

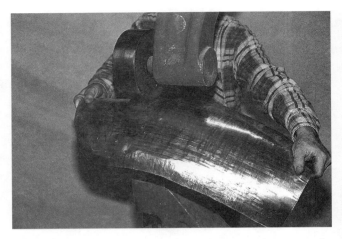

The wheel is used again, the short way, in order to stretch the metal and also minimize the walnuts left from the plastic hammer.

Wrinkles on the side indicate an excess of material, so Bo shrinks along both sides.

Note how far the metal has come. Progress is slow but steady.

Stretch and shrink, stretch and shrink. Here Bo does more stretching all through the center of the new fender.

Bo does more hammer work at the front of the fender to further stretch the metal at that point.

Bo shows the spot where he needs to lift more metal at the apex of the fender, the "top" of the fender. A little more hammer work raises this area. After the hammering Bo wheels the fender again.

"You're trying to do everything at once," says Bo, "and it's hard. As you stretch it in one direction it wants to pick up the edges in the other direction, so it's fighting you. You need to control the metal and how it moves."

Time now for another test fit, which indicates the fender needs still more shape at the very front, which brings Bo to the familiar pattern: Hammer, wheel (to take out the lumps and add to the stretch) then check the fit. Then hammer, wheel and check again. Like most of these projects, the progress here comes slowly, and at times there seems to be no progress at all.

At this point Bo puts the fender in the wheel the long way and wheels mostly at the front half of the emerging fender.

The shape is close now, but there's still not quite enough crown. "We need to lift it up here in the middle," explains Bo. The hammer is used to stretch and lift the metal followed by another session on the wheel. "You could do most of this work with the wheel," explains Bo, "but it's faster to use the hammer and the bag of sand."

Bo just keeps at it: hammer, wheel, test fit, then more hammer work. "The closer you get the harder it becomes," explains the craftsman. "And unforeseen things always seem to happen near the end."

The piece fits fairly well now, but doesn't match the contour of the buck at the end and along the sides of the piece. It's close but the sides don't wrap down tight enough. "so we'll shrink the edges, the sides more," says Bo.

Bo shrinks the nose, just to either side of the centerline and then feels for low spots. Next it's time to put the project back in the wheel and run the low spots between the two wheels, "and the low areas lift right up."

Now Bo puts it back on the wheel again because the sides still aren't down, especially in

*After a short session on the wheel it's time for Bo to do another test fit.*

*Bo does more hammering at the front of the fender and then moves to the wheel, all to create enough dome at the "top" of the fender.*

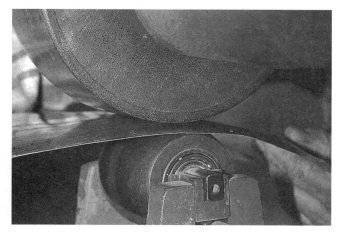

*Close up shows the large diameter upper and crowned anvil wheel.*

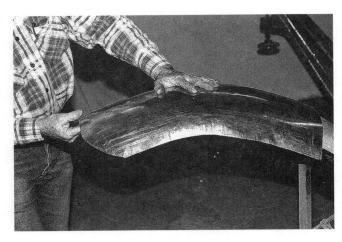

*After the smoothing and stretching of the wheel Bo does another test fit.*

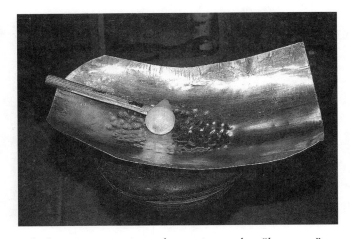

*The hammer comes into play again, used to "hump up" the area at the top of the fender.*

*After a quick test fit it's back to the wheel, running the fender through the long way.*

the corner, so "I stretch the area above it and that forces the sides down, the metal is essentially trapped."

Bo wheels it the short way next, "to hump it up higher," then runs it through the wheel the long way. "This is the frustrating part of the project," adds Bo. "When it's almost there but moving very slowly. Progress in one direction often yields a back step in the other direction." In order to get the sides to pull down more Bo goes back to the shrinker with the long sides of the fender. Then it's time to the hump the upper surface up more with the plastic hammer

It's that same old scenario, shrink and stretch, shrink and stretch.

"You can't get your shrinker way into the middle of the panel," explains Bo. "It only works at the edge, so you have to do the bulk of the shaping with stretching."

Even with all that shrinking the sides still don't come down quite tight enough. So Bo brings the fender over to the sand bag and hammers right at the edge of the "top" surface, right where the fender turns down along the side. This really causes the sides to come down tight. "I wonder in hind sight," says Bo, "if I could have made it move a lot faster earlier by using the hammer more at the very beginning."

Now the shape is nearly correct, even the sides are close, "though the nose still needs to come down a little bit," says Bo. Another run through the wheel smoothes out the walnuts, then Bo rolls it over to check the fit one more time.

After another assessment session Bo declares that we're close to finished. The only problem is the nose, it's not down tight enough against the old fender. So Bo shrinks the front corners, where Bo's finger is pointing in the picture.

The nose *still* isn't pulled down tight enough so Bo does more shrinking, but at the sides of the fender this time, near the front, which pulls the nose down tighter. Almost to the end now he raises some metal at the nose, just in from the lip on the inside, and smoothes out the lumps from hammering with the wheel.

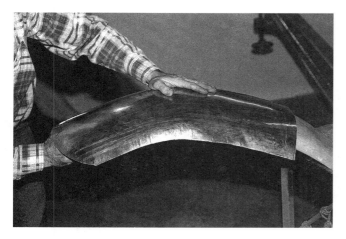

Most of the shape is here. Bo reaches his hand up under the fender to ensure the fender fits tight against the "buck."

To pull the nose down more Bo shrinks each front corner.

The shrinker is used to bring the sides in tighter.

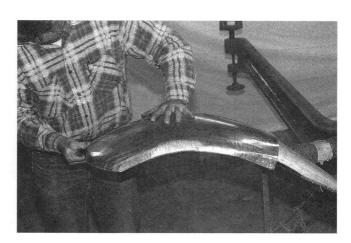

Now another test fit to check that the nose is down tight against the fender underneath.

Then it's time for another test fit.

To raise the top of the fender further, Bo stretches the area by passing it back and forth through the wheel.

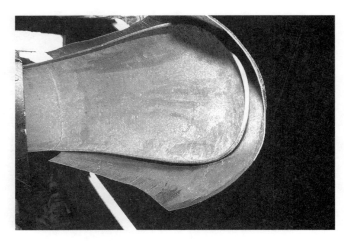

*Bottom view shows how far the edges still have to suck in to meet the buck.*

*Shrink, shrink, shrink.*

*And a little more hammer-stretching in the center of the fender.*

Now it's very nearly done.

Bo marks the edge with a marker and trims away the excess metal. Normally he would leave a half inch of extra material and wrap that around the edge wire. But in this case we will get it close to done and then call it finished.

### INTERVIEW: BO OLSON

*Bo, Can we have a little background, how you learned to do sheet metal and fabrication work?*

I learned it doing body work on old cars where the parts were unavailable. The project had to be done so you end up making the parts. It started out with a Bently convertible. I needed a rear fender and you could not buy one. So I made the whole fender, never did that before. That was hard, but not as hard you think. After a while things started to fall into place. I learned then you have to lay out a plan, where the fender's coming from and where it's going. It has to look right and fit. Not just bolt on but fit with the rest of the panels.

Then other projects came along, making fenders, hoods and parts for airplanes. I guess if you really want to finish the project you find a way. Sometimes you look at it and wonder if you should even do it. After you get into the project it usually works out. If the part doesn't work out, throw it away and try again. Sooner or later it works out.

*What tools do you consider essential to the metal shaping trade?*

The machinery you need to reproduce sheet metal parts is kind of difficult to come across. If you don't have the right equipment it's hard to create the body parts, strictly working on a sand bag with a hammer. You do need a sand bag, but you also need a wheeling machine, and a shrinking and stretching machine. And I guess you have to be able to weld the panels together.

*If you had a student, what are the basic skills you would teach them before turning them loose on a fabrication project?*

Shrinking and stretching, and the welding process in aluminum and steel. And I guess shaping metal, shaping aluminum on the sand bag. Then lots of practice on the wheeling machine.

They have to understand you have to have an eye for shape and compound curves. You may have to work off a blue print, you might have to make a buck for a fender that's a mirror image of the one on the car.

To do all that you have to be able to see that finished object in your mind. And then when you have an eye for it, you can just look over at the part you're trying to reproduce, you don't have to check it against the buck every time.

*On our fender project you used the hammer and sandbag, and the wheel, in a kind of partnership. Can you talk about how you use the two tools?*

The sand bag is stretching the metal faster. But the wheeling machine creates your shape. Your wheeling machine is creating the long flowing shapes you're after. It leaves smooth metal, it flows things out into shapes. You're using it to move the metal slower, you're nursing it into shape. The wheel is softer in the way it moves the metal. It leaves more of a finished product.

*When people make mistakes on fabrication projects, where do they go wrong?*

Not enough practice. Good technique comes with

*Another shot of the bottom shows that things are improving dramatically.*

*The amazing thing is the ability of the metal to repeatedly go from smooth to very lumpy and back to smooth, picking up more shape each time it does so.*

*Bo takes out the walnuts with the wheel.*

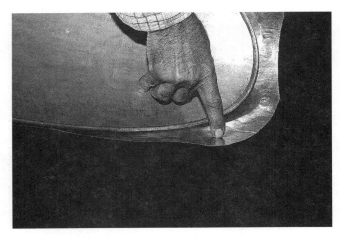
*But he still needs to pull the front corners down tighter.*

*And another round of shrinking along the sides at the front.*

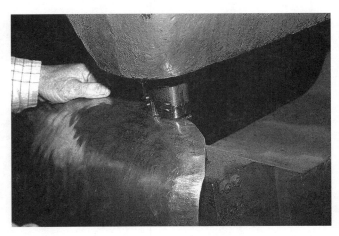
*The shrinker is employed to pull in the corners.*

*Nearly finished now, Bo uses the plastic hammer to stretch the metal at the very front.*

*Then it's time for another test fit.*

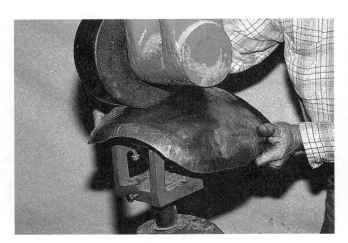
*After the last round of hammering Bo runs the fender through the English wheel one more time.*

time. The key is to do it and see what you can do, how far can you go. Then you should be able to do it a second time. The skill is in producing that part and understanding it well enough that you can do it a second time. The art of it is being able to produce the mirror image of what you just made. Whether it's a piece of an airplane or a classic car.

*Any final words of wisdom for a beginning fabricator?*

Well, the art of metal shaping, it's interesting, it's fun. You're doing something that not too many people are able to do. I think about the coach builders and the cars they built. I'm inspired by things that are hand made, whether it's a stone wall or a hand built one-off car body.

You meet interesting people and each project is different. This is very satisfying when you're done and the piece fits right and the customer is happy. You've helped to get this project out of the barn and on the street. Even though the part isn't original it's made by hand, you did the project justice and the car is done. The person is able to enjoy it. It's great to see that. You helped put it back on the road or in the air.

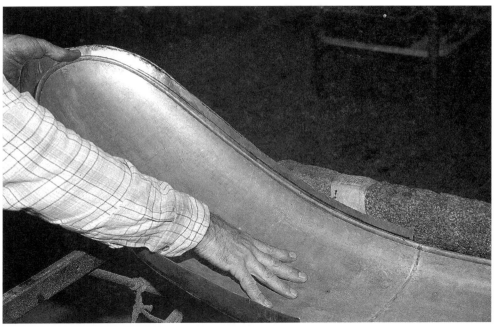

*In most cases Bo would roll the edge over a piece of "edge wire" but for this demonstration he will simply trim the metal along the marked line.*

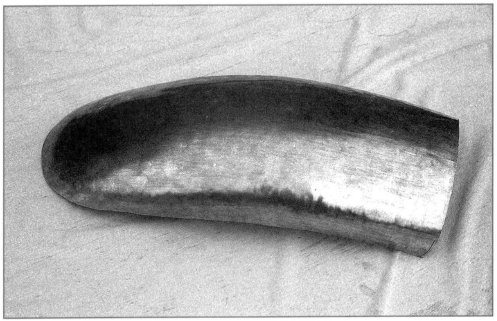

*Perhaps not fully "metal finished" this is the fender that started out only 5 or 6 hours ago as a flat piece of aluminum.*

## Chapter Eight

# A Simple Scoop

## The Importance of the Mock Up

Most of the projects shown in this book involve the actual shaping of metal, the creation of compound curves either with hand tools, large power tools or the English wheel. The creation of the blower scoop seen here is done primarily by simply bending the metal. The end cap, however, is a shaped piece with a compound curve. Anyone wanting to build a similar piece in the simplest way possible could just weld a flat piece across the back of the scoop.

*The creation of the blower scoop seen here would make a good first-time fabrication project. Unlike some other projects seen in this book, this one can be done with little or no shrinking and stretching.*

The scoop is the creation of Neal Letourneau, the same man responsible for the welding sequence in Chapter Three. Instead of power hammers or big commercial brakes, Neal did most of the necessary bending for this project with a homemade "brake" consisting of some one-inch pipe clamped to the edge of the bench.

## THE SCOOP

A Neal explains, "You need to start with a picture of something you like. Then maybe sketch the part you want with the right proportions and the dimensions drawn in. You might want to do a full-size drawing."

## THE MOCK UP

Once he has a drawing Neal starts by building-ing a full-size mock-up of the scoop from light poster board. "Be sure to put in a centerline," adds Neal, "as a reference." Neal makes the mock-up out of two pieces, the same as the actual scoop, and marks up all the lines where the bends will occur. "I even go so far as to 'form' the mock-up over a pipe," explains Neal, "to make the mock up as accurate as possible. It should be a fair representation of what you're going to do."

Before rushing from mock up to the finished piece Neal advises fabrica-

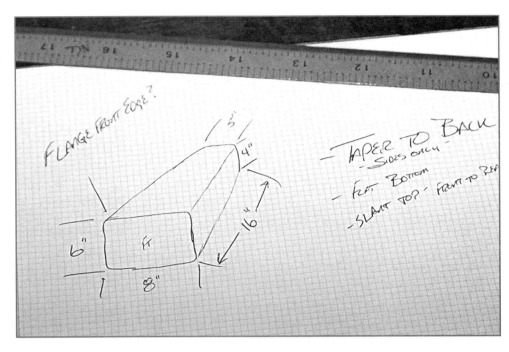

*Neal starts out with sketch of the scoop, based on a photograph of a scoop he saw in a magazine.*

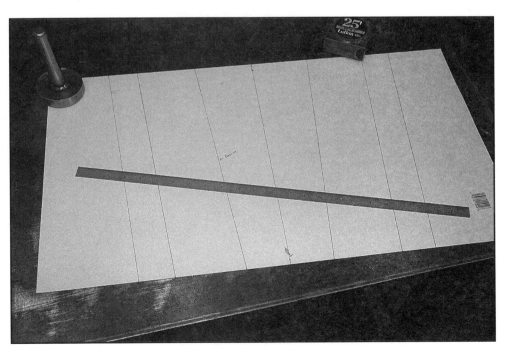

*Once he knows the size Neal transfers the dimensions to the white poster board.*

Though it seems too elaborate, Neal bends up the mock up exactly like he will the real scoop, so the mock up will truly represent the finished scoop.

The sheet of aluminum is marked, not only with the dimensions, but also the center of each bend.

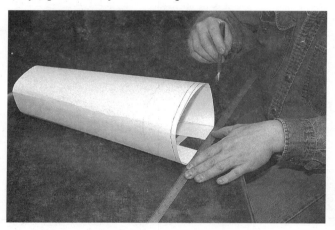

After bending up the finished mock, Neal cuts off the excess metal at the bottom of the scoop opening. The finished mock up should be as close to the actual product as possible.

A piece of one inch pipe and a few clamps are used to turn the bench into a brake.

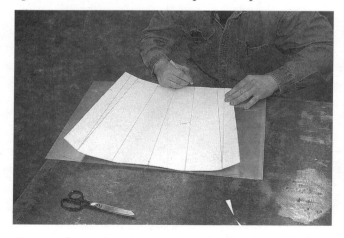

Because the mock up is accurate in its dimensions Neal can open it up and use it as a template to mark the aluminum sheet.

The pipe measures one inch O.D., so a mark is made 1/2 inch from the edge, that line is matched up to the center line for each bend. The pipe is then set flush with the edge.

tors to take a minute to asses what it is they're trying to build. "Tape up the mock up and then stand back to see if this new piece is what you want, does it fit, does it work, is it what you had in mind."

Because the mock up was cut accurately, Neal can now use it as a template to cut the material for the actual part. "Even though the material may not be real expensive," adds Neal, "the paper is cheaper. Make as many blower scoops, or whatever it is you're building, as you want from poster board until you've got one you really like."

The material being used here is .062inch, 3003 aluminum, which Neal says is a little bit heavier than it needs to be and also about the heaviest material you want to try and bend by hand. Now Neal transfers the dimensions of the mock up or template to the metal.

"It's always easier to bend *with* the grain of the material," explains Neal. "So we've laid it out and cut the material so we are in fact bending with the grain."

*With everything positioned correctly and clamped in place Neal makes the first bend.*

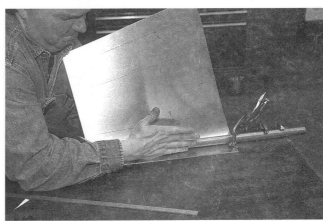

*Even though the sheet is aluminum, the .063inch material is difficult to bend. Note how both the pipe and the sheet are clamped to the bench.*

*Once the two outside bends are created Neal repositions the sheet and the pipe to make the first of the inner bends.*

## USE OF THE
## HOMEMADE BRAKE

Neal starts marking the metal by first transferring the centerline from the template to the metal. After the pattern is laid out on the material he cuts off the excess metal on either end. Now Neal needs to figure out which of the bends to bend first, second, and so on.

In order to get each bend exactly where he wants it Neal takes a couple of extra steps during

*The inner bends are somewhat more difficult to form, as the operator has less leverage to do the bending.*

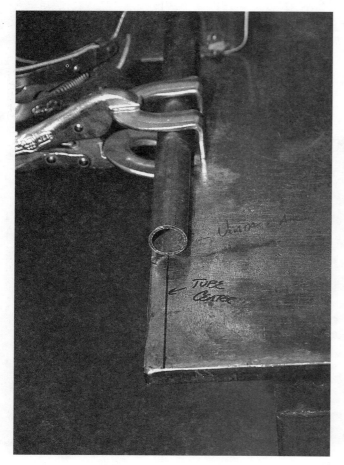

*Here you can see how the bench is marked so that by placing the pipe flush with the edge, the center of the pipe is over the line on the bench.*

the layout and bending. First, Neal marks a line on the bench that's 'half the diameter of the tube' away from the edge of the bench (check the photos to eliminate confusion). The centerline of each bend is marked on the metal to be bent. When he's ready to start bending Neal lines up the centerline on the metal with the centerline on the bench, and then positions the pipe so it's flush with the edge of the bench (this isn't nearly as complex as it sounds). All in all it's just a good, simple way to ensure the bends end up exactly where he wants them to be.

The bends must be done in sequence, so as not to create a situation where one bend prevents Neal from making the next bend.

Before making the first bend, and in fact those that come after, Neal is very careful to clamp both the pipe and the sheet metal to the bench. In this way he ensures that neither the sheet metal or the pipe can move once he starts the bending.

Once the two outside bends are completed Neal repositions the sheet and bends up first one, and then the second inner bend.

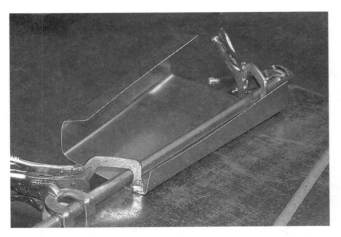

Only one bend to go. Note how one of the earlier bends wasn't a full 90 degrees and will have to be adjusted later.

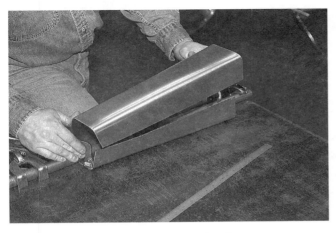

Nearly done, Neal finished the last bend.

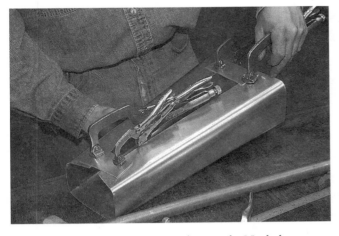

To give the scoop some structural strength, Neal clamps straps across the bottom....

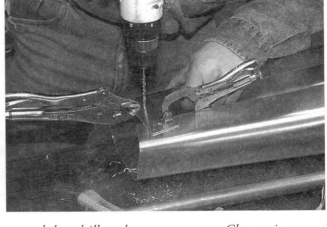

... and then drills each strap to accept a Cleco spring-loaded rivet.

Here you can see the special pliers used to install the Clecos.

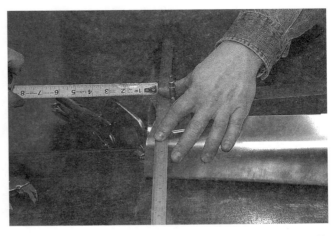

Before making the end cap Neal carefully makes a line all the way around the back of the scoop.

When it's all done Neal does a little hand "adjusting," to get everything squared up.

The new scoop is open on the bottom and doesn't have much structural strength, so Neal uses Cleco temporary rivets to hold two straps across the bottom of the scoop.

Next, Neal carefully marks the back of the scoop and then uses the tin snips to cut the back end off flush.

At this point Neal pass-

*With a high quality tin snips ("cheap tools are just cheap tools") Neal cuts the excess metal off the back of the scoop body.*

es along handy tip number four: "I never cut more than about a 1/4 inch ribbon of metal with the tin snips. If it's thicker than that you can't control the cut, and the metal won't curl and you just can't do as nice a job."

**The End Cap**

To build the rear cap Neal sets the scoop over another piece of aluminum and runs a pencil around the inside of the scoop. Before cutting he adds a margin of about 1/2 inch to the outside of the line he just drew.

To shape the rear cover Neal starts by hammering the small cover over the bag of shot with a plastic hammer, explaining as he does: "I prefer the shot, it's more stable and less affected by moisture than a bag filled with sand."

Neal stretches the cap, mostly on the horizontal axis, with the plastic hammer. The idea is to give the scoop a little shape, to add some character.

Once it's close Neal re-scribes it and trims off the excess to get the size closer to what he really wants. Now he works it over a sharper die with a plastic hammer. "The plastic hammer is nice,"

*With the scoop inverted and placed on a piece of aluminum, Neal marks the I. D. He will then add to this outline to determine the initial size of the end cap.*

explains Neal, "because it doesn't mark up the part so bad."

The hard part to form of course is the corners, as Neal explains "we're going to have to shrink those down a little bit."

Now he uses another form, a T shape dolly, and a metal hammer to force the corners into shape. "The nice thing about the thicker material," adds Neal, "is that you can pile it up in one area and then just file that area smooth."

The hardest part of the whole fabrication project is the end cap. "It's hard when you're trying to coerce the thing into shape."

"For the corners we are basically forcing the material to shrink, cold shrinking it," explains Neal.

Neal gets it close to the right size, and starts to trim away the excess material. Then he adds a bit more crown with the plastic hammer and a bag of shot. With the tin snips he trims the end cap slightly, shapes it a bit more to open up the edges and then does a test fit.

After another sesssion of trimming Neal pre-

*Neal cuts the end cap along the marked line, which means it will be too big at first.*

*Neal uses the world's oldest stretching machine to stretch the end cap, working primarily the long way.*

*Initial test fit shows how much too big the end cap is. Some of the extra material will be used to form the "sides" of the cap.*

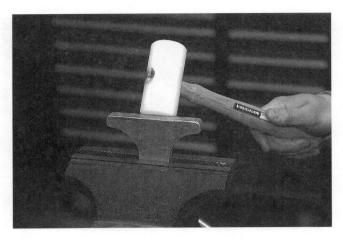

This is one of two T dollies Neal will anchor in the vise and use to shape the sides and corners of the end cap.

A change of dollies provides a small, round shape to form the corners against.

Here you can see how the hammer and dolly are used to roll the edges.

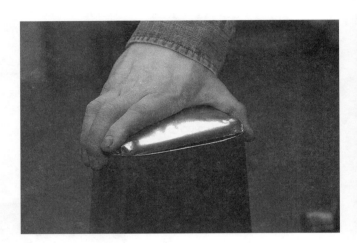

Getting closer.

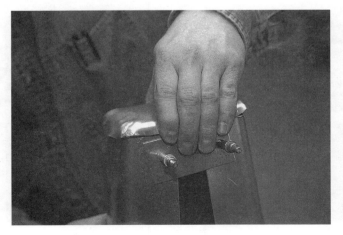

A test fit shows the end cap is still too big.

Neal stretches the end cap a bit more.

pares to tack weld the end cap to the rest of the scoop. For this task he uses 4043 rod, .060inches in diameter. The TIG welder is set on 120 amps with the high frequency adjustment set to "continuous."

First he welds the sides, then moves to the bottom. With the hammer he adjusts the fit at the top, and then tack welds that as well. Happy with the fit Neal puts down a bead all the way around the end cap.

Now that it's stuck on Neal finishes the seam, first with a Vixen file, what he describes as "the biggest, nastiest file you can find."

After the Vixen file Neal does a little work with a small power sander, and finishes up with a the "AVOS System," which consists of a backing plate and Scotch Brite pads intended to fit the small sander. The nice thing about this system is the "holes" in the pads and the backing palte (see the illustration in Chapter Two) that allow you to actually "see" the metal through the spin-

*Near the end Neal uses this highly specialized tool to pull the sides out just a little.*

*First a few tack welds.*

*Then a little adjusting where the scoop doesn't quite meet the edge of the end cap.*

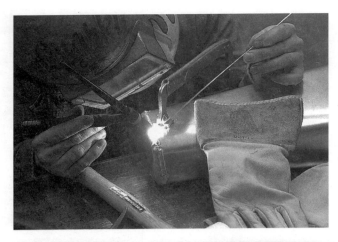

*Neal does a bead all the way around the end cap with the TIG welder.*

*The finished end cap, before the filing and sanding.*

ning disc. And of course because the pads are made of Scotch Brite material, they're only mildly abrasive and not likely to damage or overheat the aluminum.

We could go farther, but the Scotch Brite pads leave the new scoop in reasonably good condition. For here it would noramlly be a matter of cutting out part of the bottom to fit the carburetors before finishing or polishing the entire blower scoop.

The beauty of this little demonstration is twofold: First, note the importance of the mock up and its use as a template. Even when building very simple projects it's a very good idea to build it from paper first. Second, note the fact that, except for the end cap, the whole thing was created with nothing more than a sheet of aluminum, a bench, a piece of pipe and a few vise grips.

*A coarse, or Vixen, file is used to knock down the worst of the bead...*

*...followed by some sanding, working first with a coarse grit pad and then a special Scotch Brite pad.*

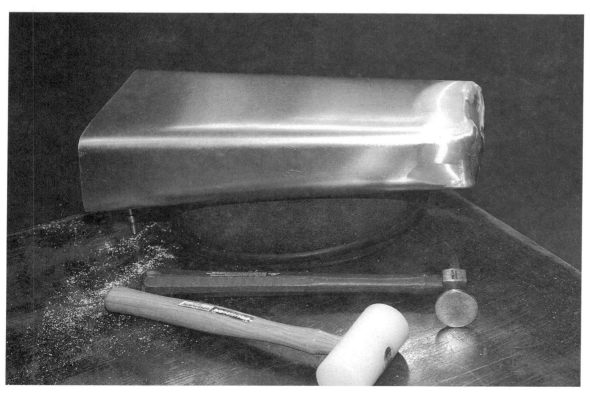

*The finished hood scoop, formed primarily with nothing more sophisticated than a piece of pipe and a little elbow grease.*

## Chapter Nine

# Wheeler Dealers

## Marcel De Ley & Sons

At the De Ley shop in Corona, California, Marcel and his two sons, Luc and Marc, fabricate a variety of panels and complete projects. One week they might be building panels that will be assembled later into a prototype car for one of the Big Three. The following week it might be repair on a Chevy street rod body or a fender for a rare old Packard or Mercedes Benz.

Luc explains that much of the work they do is for other shops, "We don't do much of the finish work, because the shops we work for have people who can

*Marcel in the center, flanked by Luc on his left and Marc on his right. Behind them is the "1934 Ford" and a variety of hot rod and restoration projects.*

do that. What we do is form the basic panels and weld them together."

It's interesting to note that Marcel never did go to school and is essentially self-taught. His first job when he came to the states was in a body shop. And over the course of the next ten years Marcel graduated from standard crash repair to the restoration of very rare, very expensive European automobiles.

## WHEELING A DOOR SKIN:

The demonstration project shown here is the creation of a raw door skin. Though most of us would assume the English wheel is the best tool for a job like this, Marcel and Luc show us one of the tricks they've learned after forming panels for over 20 years.

Instead of just taking the sheet of 18 gauge cold-rolled steel to the English wheel, they first take it over to the Eckold hammer equipped with a set of shrinking dies. They explain that by shrinking the edges along the long side of the panel, the whole job will go much faster. "It starts the shape forming very quickly," explains Luc. "The Eckold is also a good way to make the curve 'fatter,' or more crowned, in only one part of a panel like a door skin. A good example would be a door skin that rolls in more steeply at the top than it does at the bottom."

After shrinking both of the long edges of the panel Marcel and Luc move to the English wheel. The anvil wheel that Luc and Marcel use has almost no crown. "I've seen people use more rounded wheels," says Luc. "But the contact area gets so small that they can put creases in the metal. You want each pass through to overlap slightly with the last, you really can't do that with the narrow

*Our little demonstration project starts with a raw piece of sheet steel that will make a good outer door skin for this sedan.*

*To speed up the shaping, Luc and Marcel shrink the long edges of the "door skin" on the Eckold hammer equipped with shrinking dies.*

*Here you can see the sheet has already picked up some crown, just from the shrinking.*

*To put the real crown in the door skin Luc and Marcel run the whole thing through the English wheel.*

wheels. This is a stretching operation, you want a pretty flat set of wheels."

With Marcel on one end of the panel and Luc on the other they start the panel between the two wheels and roll it back and forth the long way. As Luc explained, each pass overlaps the last one just slightly. When they've reached the other side of the panel it's removed from the English wheel so they can examine the degree of crown they've achieved. As you can see from the photos, in only one "pass" through the English wheel the panel has picked up a fair amount of crown.

The trick here is to make a compound curve, to make it move the right amount in two axis. "We could have done this with the wheel totally," says Luc. "But it was easier and faster to do it with the two tools together." Luc goes on to explain that though some wheels are hardened the wheels they use are not.

The De Ley family did a fair amount of work on the Chevy sedan seen in the photos (also seen in an earlier chapter). The hardest part of the project was the creation of the rear panel. This is a difficult piece to make because of the reverse curve. Looking at this panel from the back of the car, it is concave in a horizontal axis and convex on the vertical axis. It's hard to get the metal to go in two different directions. Luc and Marcel created the panel by rolling the edges, not the center, with the English wheel. With the paper taped in place you can see how the metal had to stretch at the edges to form the correct shape.

The other interesting project in their shop is what Luc calls the "modern version" of a '34 Ford. Provided with only a side view of the car, and a rolling chassis, the De Ley family crafted everything else from scratch. Luc explains that the car is made from a variety of materials, "The floors are 16 gauge steel while the fenders and much of the body is 18 gauge. Some of that is Aluminum killed and some is just plain cold-rolled steel. The hood is aluminum and the trim is carved from a strip of solid brass.

## INTERVIEW, LUC DE LEY

*Luc, Can we start with a little background on you and your father?*

We've been doing this for 24 years. My Father Marcel is self taught. He emigrated here from Belgium in the early 1960s, and at that time there was no call for this kind of work so Dad did regular body work. Sometimes, though, a Ferrari would come in the shop and they couldn't get any parts. So Dad would build a nose cone or a fender for the car. Eventually he built a reputation for that kind of work and that's all he did. We opened our own shop in 1975 in Orange county

*Note the relatively large diameter of the upper wheel, and the fact that the lower, or anvil, wheel has almost no crown at all.*

and seven years ago we moved out here.

*Luc, how much of the work we see in the shop is done with the wheel?*

99 percent the work you see is done with the English wheel.

*How long did it take you to learn your trade?*

I did it for 15 years before I felt comfortable making panels from scratch by myself. I think I started to learn more when Dad took longer vacations and I couldn't ask him for help. It's hard to teach this to someone else because you don't always know exactly what, or how, you're doing what you're doing.

Building panels from scratch, it's a hard trade, it's not like being a machinist. There are so many ways to go with any particular project. There are a number of different tools, and different methods, you can use even with the same tool.

*So it's not essential to use an English wheel like you do or a power hammer like Steve Davis does?*

*Each pass through the wheel overlaps he last just slightly. It takes strength and concentration to move a large sheet like this through the wheel in a controlled fashion.*

*Here you can see the marks left by the shrinker, and the crown the piece picked up with only one pass through the English wheel.*

*With the ruler turned 90 degrees, it's obvious the piece is crowned in two axis - a compound curve.*

*Though it isn't finished, the demonstration shows how a typical door skin, or roof insert, might be formed from scratch.*

No, we used that old tree stump for a long time and sometimes we still use it to shape small parts or small areas on larger panels. We started out using the English wheel just to take the "walnuts" out of what we'd done. But over time we get better and better with the wheel. The nice thing about the wheel is that when you're done making something with the English wheel you don't have to spend a lot of time taking the walnuts out of it.

*So you learned most of your skills from your Father?*

Yes, for 24 years I've been connected to my Dad through the piece of steel. I've been on the other side of all those panels.

*What's the hardest part of scratch building like you do?*

The hardest part is learning how to get started. Sometimes it helps to do a mock up with a piece of paper. Then you realize you can't shrink or stretch it that far, or you aren't comfortable stretching it that far. Which means you're going to have to make it out of two or more pieces. I use more pieces when I want to be more accurate. It might take me an extra 15 minutes to weld together two pieces, as opposed to an extra 2 hours to work with a piece that's twice that big.

For example, the way we build '32 Ford decklids, we build them with a seam in the middle running across, for us it's just much faster that way. Basically, we do production work so there's always the challenge of doing it in the fastest way possible.

*Do you always use a buck when you're making large pieces?*

Yes, and the buck must be stronger than the piece of steel. Even though you aren't really forming the part over the buck, it must be strong enough that you can clamp the piece to it and maybe lean on the sheet metal when it's located on the buck.

We don't do real fine finish work. When we're done you can probably still see the seams. We do fabrication work for other shops. They can do the metal finishing or the skin coat of plastic, but not the shaping. They do the finish work themselves. Sometimes we take the project to the point where a painter can finish it, it's up to our customer.

*Can we talk a bit about the advantages and disadvantage of steel and aluminum?*

I like working with aluminum more, it's lighter to handle and forms quicker, but it's not as forgiving. With steel, it's easier to weld, you can put lead on a edge. Nobody wants Bondo on these cars, it's OK though to use lead. Of course that only works on steel. And the hammer and dolly work goes twice as fast on aluminum. For guys at home, steel is probably easier, just because of the welding aspect. It's harder for most welders to weld aluminum.

*What about welding, do you do gas or heli-arc welding when you join these panels?*

Our welding is all done with heli-arc. We use heli-arc to avoid any corrosion at the weld. After welding we run the bead through the roller or we hammer and dolly the bead. Heli-arc is faster and cleaner. A gas-welded bead has the advantage of being a little bit softer and easier to work.

*How heavy is the steel you use to repair and build these old bodies?*

The floors are 16 gauge, most body panels are 18 or 19 gauge. We try to always use drawing-quality steel. We order a whole bunch at a time, you have to ask for drawing quality sheet. The commercial grade cold rolled steel isn't always the same stuff. The way to judge the softness of a certain sheet of steel is to bend over a corner of a sheet, between your thumb and forefinger. If it springs back then it's pretty stiff and will be harder to work.

*How about one really good piece of advice for beginning metal shapers?*

Don't be afraid to make a mistake. This is not magic. People look at this as being so special. Don't be afraid to throw something away Don't be afraid to try something new. You don't have to be too careful, be aggressive, it's tough to do a piece and have it look really nice when you're in the middle of forming something. Usually it looks like a bag of walnuts, it looks like hell. But once you have the shape you can clean it up with the hammer and dolly or the wheel, and it will usually turn out fine.

Don't expect to learn this overnight. You learn these skills by doing it over and over and throwing some stuff away. I've only known a couple of guys who caught on real quick. So just go out and pick up a hammer and give it a try.

*What's the best part of being able to build all these panels from scratch?*

I get a real satisfaction when I'm done. I like to stand back and look at what I've done, not very many people can do what we do here.

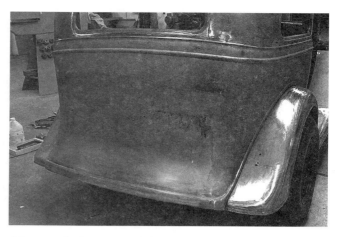

*The rear body section of the coupe, a piece that is essentially concave and convex at the same time.*

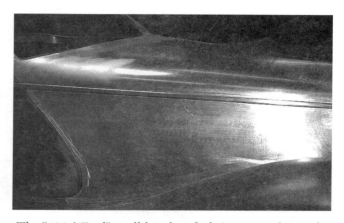

*The "1934 Ford" is all hand crafted. Some panels are aluminum killed steel while much of the car is cold-rolled 18 and 19 gauge steel. The strip running the car's length is solid brass, which will be plated later.*

*The complete car waiting for final finishing by another shop. The whole thing was fabricated to fit an existing chassis, based on an artist's renderings.*

## Chapter Ten

# The "English Wheel"

## The Work of John Reed

John Reed is the sometimes invisible designer of many aftermarket Harley-Davidson parts seen in the huge Custom Chrome catalog. Though he might not seem like a sheet metal fabricator at first glance, many of John's prototypes, the ones

he takes to the product meetings at Custom Chrome, are sheet metal pieces shaped using simple one-off forms based loosely on the finished production tooling. As John explains, "I went through a formal apprenticeship in England. I

*John Reed, surrounded by machines of his own creation, including the "Street Fighter" V-Twin motorcycle. John* *designed and fabricated his own frame built from large-diameter mild-steel tubing.*

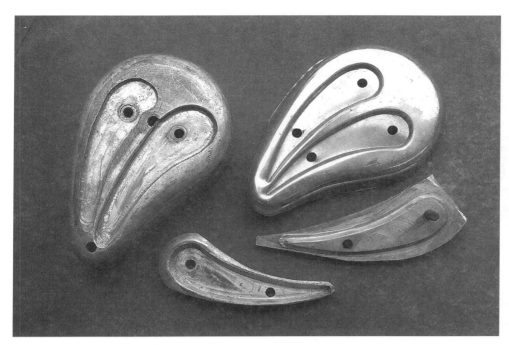

On the left, an air cleaner plug formed from aluminum with the two small male inserts on the bottom. On the right, the prototype air cleaner.

a second skin. I know that if I form it deeper than the final trim line, the part can be made from production tooling. And if the shape is exactly the same as the plug, the toolmaker can digitize the plug and production will exactly match the dimensions of my prototype to a few thousandths of an inch."

The sequence starts with material choice. John often uses 6061 aluminum. It is harder to

was indentured for 6 years to the Atomic Research Authority's establishment at Harwell."

"Sheet metal work isn't difficult if you have invested the time and learn how to do it right. I was taught the basic skills of sheet metal work when I was an apprentice, that was nearly 40 years ago. I still use the first hammer that I ever beat a piece of metal with, and I am still not sure I've mastered it.

"I have to produce a production quality prototype similar to my initial sketches, which have been approved by the Custom Chrome product selection committee. And the only accurate way of doing this, while maintaining the curves designed in the initial three-dimensional rendering, is by using the small tooling shapes you see 'round my shop."

"It is a process which gets simpler with each shape I make out of aluminum or steel. But instead of a female die, and a controlling plate, I hammer the part over the male plug, holding up the metal edge while shrinking and stretching the metal close to the plug so it follows the plug like

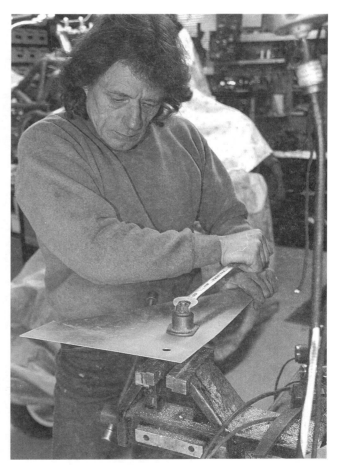

By drawing the two piece tooling together (shown on the next page) John creates a neat dimple in the sheet metal.

form (than the softer aluminum alloys) and he has to anneal it many times during the shaping process, but it has a spring that's closer to steel.

John has figured out many methods of changing a flat piece of material into a complex shape that has the appeal for the retail customer to buy in quantities sufficient to justify the considerable investment in high quantity production tooling. Sometimes it is easier to press the prototype with the small 14 ton press in

*John's tooling is nothing more than a male and female die and a connecting bolt.*

*Here you see John work a piece of aluminum sheet down over one of the plugs (using it as a hammer form) machined from a billet of aluminum.*

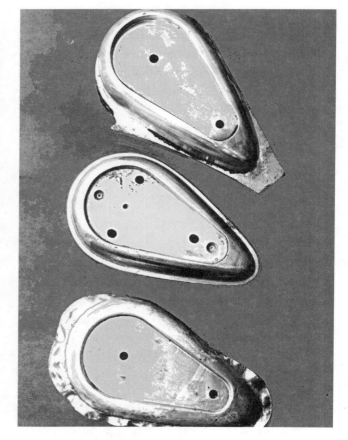

*Top: the first raw plug. Middle: the production tooling. Bottom: The first prototype part, formed by hammering the aluminum over the form.*

134

the corner of the shop, rather than hand form it.

"The process is really rather simple," explains John. "But you must have an edge, a flat section at the edge of the taper (on the tooling) so you control the edge of the sheet metal just outside of the tool. You must have control the metal outside of the male and female die."

"Many times you get wrinkles in the metal outside the dies, after the part is pressed or formed. That's because you're stretching the metal in the dies, so there's some "extra" metal left over, outside the dies. When you have too much metal it wrinkles."

""You need to be a bit analytical when you do sheet metal work like this, you need reference marks always, a center line or a pair of holes for some dowel pins. People want to just start out working free-form and you really can't do it that way."

Most of John's methods are based on his understanding of the forces required to change a flat piece of sheet metal into one of the complex shapes required by the retail buyer. Much of the prototype press tooling

*Male and female dies created in John's shop to form small triangular impressions in sheet metal.*

*Here we see a piece of raw aluminum set up in the press with the two dies.*

*With the press opened up John removes the upper die.*

*Wrinkles along the edge indicate an excess of material, which John shrinks away with the shrinking hammer.*

*A variety of shrinking tools, including two curved files and two hammers. The hammer on the left, the one used above, utilizes a cam-actuated rotating head to gather up the metal under the head with each blow.*

*Once the polishing starts the low spots show up dark. John raises these from the back side with a very small hammer.*

seen in John's shop is based on the principles of the production tooling, i.e. forcing a male shape into a female shape of either aluminum or steel or urethane, while holding the edge up and controlling its flow into the ever diminishing gap. The sheet metal must stretch and shrink itself into an exact replica of the prototype.

After pre-shaping on a press the prototype has to be polished and finished so it looks like its mass-produced clones. Unlike the replicated ancestors, however, the prototype continues to demand the dedicated attention of a craftsman.

After being formed, the part is hand trimmed and then smoothed with a DA sander starting with a 80 grit pad, if it is real rough, working down in steps to a 360 grit pad. Whenever a high or low spot is found, John stops and dresses it out with that same old tired hammer on a carefully ground anvil.

As the abrasives get finer and the finish gets smoother John changes from the bees-wax type lubricant, available from Eastwood, to Solvol Autosol. This German metal polish is one of John's favorites for working on aluminum and many alloys.

Eventually the part takes on a chrome-like sheen. It's then a matter of using finer and finer abrasive rolls, and other assorted smaller and smaller, faster and faster revolving abrasives. These rolls come in a multitude of sizes, shapes and compounds, so John can get into all the recesses before taking the part to the buffing wheels for the final steps from carburundom compound on a coarse spiral buffing wheel to jewelers rouge on a soft cotton finishing buff.

John obviously gets a lot of satisfaction from the finished part. And he seems to get a kick out of the huge sales numbers some of his products have generated. He enthuses openly when talking of the huge sales quantities of parts he has designed and prototyped in the past.

After all these years John's only regret is the possible harm he's done to himself through lack of safety equipment. This helps to explain his current emphasis on dust masks and charcoal filters when buffing, especially on aluminum.

*The polishing starts with a 80 grit pad on a DA, lubricated with bee's wax, and quickly moves to finer abrasive pads and eventually the large polishing wheels and buffs.*

*The final piece, polished to an almost chrome-like finish before being "scuffed" to the final satin finish.*

## Chapter Eleven

# Old-World Attitude

## Cass Nawrocki

Cass Nawrocki is a man who hates to do the same job twice. After nearly 30 years of fabricating and metal finishing Cass still finds the work challenging, perhaps because he's always taking new and different projects into his shop in Moose Lake, Minnesota.

When Cass emigrated here from Communist Poland in 1969, his first job was at a body shop. Despite the fact that he had no training in body work Cass quickly learned the ins and outs of crash

*Though Cass Nawrocki started as a conventional body man he quickly learned the skills necessary for restoration and fabrication. Today Cass creates everything from antique motorcycle fenders to complete classic cars.*

repair and Bondo application. Three years later Cass secured a job in a restoration shop in the Phoenix area. At this new shop cars were finished with a "pick and file" instead of a Bondo bucket and sanding block.

Never content for long, Cass opened his own shop in 1978 doing restoration and fabrication work. Once Cass learned how to restore old parts he moved on to the fabrication of new parts that were no longer available. From there he made the next logical step, the fabrication of complete bodies.

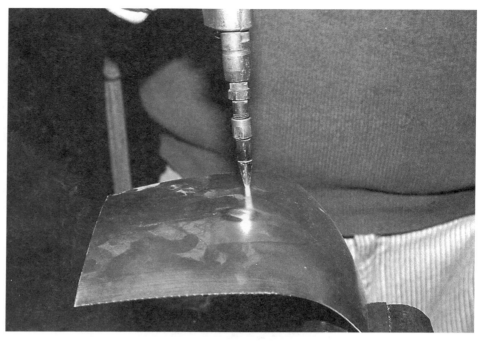

*The key to heat shrinking steel is to heat only one small dime-size spot. Then cool it quickly.*

The photo albums in Cass' office are filled with success stories. Stories like the fabrication of two complete Mercedes 540Ks and a 1932 Lincoln. When he says he made the whole body, he means everything, even the trim and bumpers. The big romantic projects tend to overshadow all the smaller jobs that have gone in and out of the shop over the years. Jobs like creating slant-noses for Porsches, restoring old Packards or Auburns, and building modern street rods. Though other shop owners might look forward to repetitive work as a way to make more money, or effectively raise the hourly rate, Cass retains his aversion to doing the same job twice. When he does get a request for ten bumpers for a rare Mercedes, the challenge shifts from fabricating the part, to fabricating the tooling necessary to do a short production run of the obscure parts.

Cass' understanding of tooling, and his willingness to

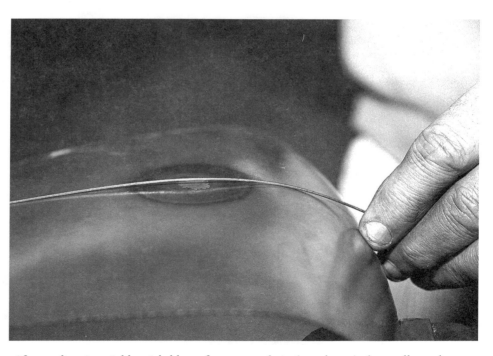

*After cooling it quickly with blast of compressed air (not shown) the small spot has indeed shrunk. Cass advises first-time heat shrinkers to use caution to avoid over shrinking the panel.*

To make the outer mirror housing for a Porsche, Cass first took a fiberglass mold off an existing mirror (seen on the left) and used that to pour the male die from concrete.

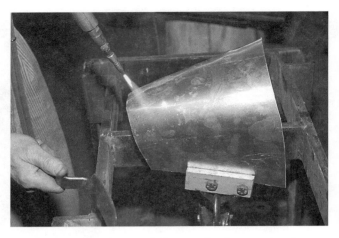

With tension on the panel Cass applies heat to the aluminum and then forces the metal to shrink with a slapper.

With the die mounted on the rack, Cass positions the sheet aluminum that will make up the new mirror body.

As the mirror housing takes shape, Cass trims away excess metal.

Come-alongs are clamped onto each end of the raw aluminum and then anchored to the lower part of the rack.

Encouraged with the slap hammer and heat, the small end of the housing is taking shape.

More work with the slapper and more heat, all while keeping tension on the aluminum. The aluminum is being forced to conform to the small end of the die.

Once the piece is finished on the from, Cass removes it and uses the fiberglass form as a guide to trim the edges.

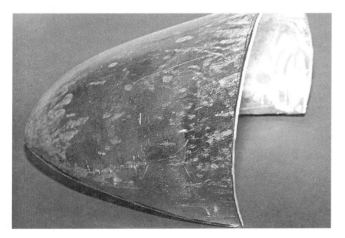

The finished mirror housing, shaped with the help of some simple, yet innovative, tooling.

Confronted with repairing a damaged aluminum cowling Cass devised some easily formed, male and female "dies" from wood to re-create each hole.

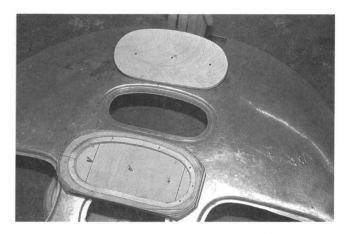

Here you can see the two dies, with copper guide pins to ensure they stay in alignment.

Adjustable clamps are used to put the squeeze on the aluminum and thus force it to follow the shape dictated by the dies.

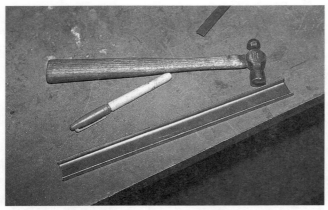

*This demonstration shows how Cass makes perfectly formed trim pieces from raw stainless steel. For our purposes the raw metal is mild steel. First the metal is bent into a U shape as shown.*

*This tooling requires two passes through the dies. Here the channel is pre-bent to get it started and inserted in the die. The clamp on the left is connected to a come-along, used to pull the channel through and do the initial forming.*

*After the first pass through the die, the channel is re-inserted as shown here. Cass considers this a good tool because, "it didn't cost us anything but a little time and it works great."*

*The second part of the die is inserted here, the channel is pulled through one more time, with plenty of lubricant, and the correctly formed channel emerges.*

spend time and effort designing tooling, is one of the things that separates him from other metal fabricators. The shop in Moose Lake, Minnesota is filled to the brim, not just with an English wheel and assorted power hammers, but with an incredible array of custom tooling. Each piece, like the male and female dies his step-son Vladimir used to form a channel that's part of a Mercedes nose assembly, is built in-house to help Cass and Vladimir fabricate some intricate shape.

Over lunch Cass explains what he feels to be the basics of nearly all fabrication. To illustrate his point he uses examples of work in his own shop, as well as the way the panels were likely formed and joined on the new Volkswagon sitting in the parking lot.

Though there are some short "how to" sequences that follow, and Cass' Nine Principles (or principle things to remember while fabricating), this chapter is primarily a shop tour of one very interesting shop in northern Minnesota.

# The Nine Principles
## as dictated by Cass Nawrocki.

Like the first law of thermodynamics, Cass has one principle that supersedes all others. And when in doubt he always refers back to his First Principle:

For every action there is a reaction. Though it sounds like first-year physics, Cass doesn't think most fabricators remember his rule. Too often they apply the hammer or shrinker to one part of a panel without realizing that their action may have effects well beyond the small area where they're working.

Number two: Protect what you can, protect the work you've already done, before going on to do more work on a panel or project.

Number three: Curved panels are easy to repair and fabricate, it's the flat ones that are difficult.

Number four: When you shrink with the torch, especially on a flat panel, do it carefully. Allow each shrink-spot to cool completely before considering any additional shrinking. Otherwise you can easily over-shrink and "oil-can" the panel.

Number five: Panels and parts, like some fenders that combine concave and convex shapes, are very difficult to shape.

Number six: Stretching is always easier than shrinking.

Number seven: Don't design in metal. Before fabricating a complete new piece be sure to create one in fiberglass or foam first. "You can start with one of the foams that shape easily," says Cass. "Use a knife or a 'cheese grater.' to carve the shape. Then in order to make it more durable or make it into a male die, you can cover it in fiberglass."

Number eight: Steel and aluminum behave very differently. You can't just take the same methods you use for steel and apply them to aluminum, you have to understand aluminum first.

Number nine: How many seams you put in a panel depends on the panel itself and the skills of the fabricator. "If you're a better welder than you are a shaper, then a small panel might be made up of ten pieces," says Cass. "If, on the other hand, you're a better fabricator than you are welder, then the same piece might be made up of only two or three."

*Another mini-demo: To start, Cass and Vladimir made a female mold from an existing nose section for a Mercedes.*

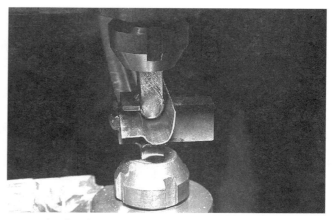

*To make the channel that is part of the front end they make a special male and female die for the Pullmax. As the male die moves up and down the correct channel is formed.*

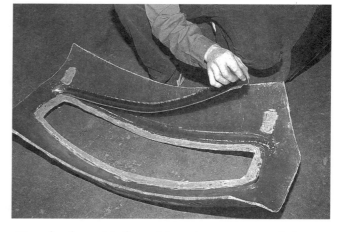

*Now the channel is formed into the correct curved shape with the use of the fiberglass female die of the entire front end.*

143

# Sources

Covell, Ron
(Ron sells a complete line of fabrication tools, books and videos
as well as small quantities of cold rolled and aluminum killed steel.)
106 Airport Blvd #210
Freedom, CA 95019
800 747 4631

Davis Cars
224 E Alton Av  unit C
Santa Ana, CA  92707

Fournier Enterprises
(They sell a complete line of fabrication tools and equipment.)
1884 Thunderbird St
Troy, MI 48084
284 362 3722

Letourneau, Neal
308 Lion Ln
Shoreview, MN 55126

Marcel's Custom Metal
1621 Commerce
Corona, CA 91720

Moal, Steve
Moal's Body Shop
937 E 12th St
Oakland CA 94606

Nawrocki, Cass
4634 So Arrowhead Lane
Moose Lake, MN 55767

Olson, Robert
Rivertown Carrozeria
114 W Churchill St.
Stillwater, MN 55082